Hunger for
HOLINESS

D0809977

word for **TODAY**

Hunger for HOLINESS

Malachi: A call to commitment today

STEPHEN GAUKROGER

SCRIPTURE UNION
130 CITY ROAD, LONDON EC1V 2NJ

© Stephen Gaukroger 1992

The right of Stephen Gaukroger to be identified as author of
this work has been asserted by him in accordance with the
Copyright, Designs and Patents Act 1988.

First published 1992
by Scripture Union, 130 City Road, London EC1V 2NJ

ISBN 0 86201 713 0

British Library Cataloguing in Publication Data
A catalogue record for this book is available from the British
Library.

Designed by Mark Carpenter Design.

Phototypeset by Input Typesetting Ltd, London.
Printed and bound in Great Britain by Cox and Wyman Ltd,
Reading.

CONTENTS

Thanks to:

- Becky, whose editorial additions are always so much better than my original offering.
- The church family in Stopsley, for their love and support.
- Some special people who work with me.
- JLM, BJ, CE, and SR, whom I love

Dedicated to:

Ray and Christine Brown – special people who gave me a hunger for biblical exposition, church history . . . and holiness!

1

A GOD COMMITTED TO HIS PEOPLE

One winter's night, a cold, exhausted tramp was found in the streets by the Salvation Army. Two of their officers half walked, half carried him back to their hostel. They sat him down on a bed, gave him a towel and some soap and suggested he might like to have a wash. Looking in on him ten minutes later, he was still sitting there, huddled up, too exhausted to move.

So they lifted him gently and carried him to the bathroom where they helped him wash. Then they took him back to the bed and tucked him in.

It's OK for God to tell us that we need to be spiritually clean, but we need help to get to that point.

Even when he's given us the soap and towel, we still don't know how to go about cleaning up our act. So he comes alongside us and works with us to bring about the results he wants to see.

GOD ENCOURAGES OUR HOLINESS

In the Boston Public Library in America there is a huge painting on one of the walls. It's a painting of all the 'minor prophets', by John Sergeant. On the far right of the painting is Malachi. It's a brilliant portrayal of him, because it manages to capture all three of the main themes of the Book of Malachi: affirmation, confrontation and anticipation.

Like the child who needs to be helped and encouraged to do what his father asks him, we can be sure of God's total involvement in all that he asks of us. As we look at the ins and outs of commitment to God in today's world, we'll discover how he helps us achieve this: he affirms his love for us; he confronts us over things that are wrong in our lives; and he reveals to us the big picture of his activity in the world, so spurring us on to bring ourselves more fully under his rule.

Affirmation

A first glance at Malachi in the Boston painting reveals a smiling, warm-natured man. As you walk past, Malachi gazes down on you benevolently, affirmingly. Affirmation was something the Israelites badly needed at the time when Malachi brought God's word to them.

In 597 BC Jerusalem was beseiged by the Babylonians. The king and many of the important officials were captured and taken away to Babylon, and the Babylonians put a puppet king in place in Jerusalem. But eleven years later, the Babylonians decided to finish the job they had started. They came back to Jerusalem in force and completely demolished it. The massacre of its citizens was appalling and those who escaped the sword were taken into captivity in Babylon.

Seventy years passed. Babylon was itself over-powered by the Persian king, Cyrus, but he made it possible for the Israelites to go back home to their ruined towns and villages. Later, under the leadership of Zerubbabel, the temple was rebuilt and, in 458 BC, many more Jews returned with Ezra the priest. In 445 BC Nehemiah returned from Persia and took charge of the rebuilding of the walls of Jerusalem.

But then, in about 433 BC, Nehemiah was recalled to Persia, and the people's confidence began to waver.

True, the people were now back from exile, but the great promises of blessing that had been made to them by prophets like Isaiah didn't seem to be materialising. The people became depressed and discouraged. 'Didn't God say he would bless us once we got back here?' they asked, '. . . but it doesn't look like there's much going for us at the moment . . .'

'Didn't God say . . . ?' is classic 'Satan talk'. In the very first temptation in the Garden of Eden, Satan sowed seeds of doubt in the couple's mind. 'Did God really say that . . . ?' he asked. 'Did he really mean that you weren't supposed to do that . . . ?' Nagging doubts, fears and questions began to erode the people's commitment to the God who had brought them back from exile. But God's first word to them through Malachi is one of love and assurance. 'I love you and I am going to fulfil my promises to you; I will never fail you.'

It is important for us to know that God's first word to us is the same. Before anything else, he loves us. When we're going through discouraging times, whether individually or as a church, he wants us to know he's going to keep his promises to us. They are as immovable as Ben Nevis and more secure than any guarantee you could get anywhere in the world. God has never failed anyone yet, and he is not going to start now! He loves us too much for that.

Confrontation

If you look back at that picture of Malachi on the wall of the Boston Library, you may see another expression. On closer examination, the prophet isn't quite as happy as you first thought. His brow is furrowed and he looks, well, a bit concerned.

There's a strength and determination behind God's love. Underlying his words of affirmation, 'Yes, I love you, my people,' is a deep concern for our holiness: '. . . and here's the reason why some things are going wrong in your life, your society, your culture. Get these principles right, and you'll be able to receive my blessing in those areas.'

We need to be confronted again today by God's holy word, individually, and as church congregations, so that our lives can be brought into line with his plans for us.

A few years ago our church spent some weeks looking at what the Bible says about social action. People are not just souls with ears, but living human beings with all sorts of physical, social and emotional needs, all of which matter to God. As we thought together about this we realised that we had to act on what God was saying in his word. We thought seriously about employing a full-time social worker – and did so. Soon we had two, linked with the Spurgeon's Childcare Project. Now the church has a social service which is respected and valued by the local secular social service organisations. When we listen, God will speak and direct our plans.

Anticipation

There's a third feature of the Boston painting. All the other prophets seem to be looking outwards, into the world, as it were. But Malachi is looking forward, straining to catch a glimpse of the future. The Book of Malachi is the last book in the Old Testament, and Malachi was the last prophet the Jews had until the coming of John the Baptist. The picture shows him looking forward to the coming of Christ, when God's promises would be fulfilled.

Malachi knew that much of the pain and suffering of God's people could not be resolved without a major intervention of God himself. So he looked forward to the day when God would affirm his love so clearly that the people would have no doubts about it at all. He also saw that this would mean the clearing out for good of all the people's unholiness, guilt and failure. He looked forward to the 'Day of the Lord' when, with God's help, his people would be made completely holy.

God often uses these three things – affirmation, confrontation and anticipation – to help us move on in our ministry, work, or the way we live our lives. When I was a student at Spurgeon's College, a church in Dallas invited me to go over there for a year's placement. At first I felt a tremendous sense of excitement, privilege and thrill. It was great to feel so affirmed and needed! But then people began to confront me with my motives. Was this going to be just a 'year out' before the 'real' work? Was it a cheap way of seeing the USA? What was I going to be able to give to that church? And then *I* began to ask questions too. What if God has got something *here*, in England, for me to do? Would I be missing out on doing his work here by disappearing off to America?

But then I found that, as I talked through all these doubts and questions with my father, I felt a growing sense of anticipation about the prospect of going to the States. He helped me see that there were lots of things I could learn, some things I could contribute, and that the call was one I should accept.

With the help of friends and family, God had

moved me through these stages of affirmation, confrontation and anticipation, to the point where I was sure that the move was the right and good one to make.

GOD AFFIRMS HIS LOVE

'An oracle: The word of the Lord to Israel through Malachi.

"I have loved you," says the Lord.

"But you ask, 'How have you loved us?'

"Was not Esau Jacob's brother?" the Lord says, "Yet I have loved Jacob, but Esau I have hated, and I have turned his mountains into a wasteland and left his inheritance to the desert jackals."

Edom may say, "Though we have been crushed, we will rebuild the ruins."

But this is what the Lord Almighty says: "They may build but I will demolish. They will be called The Wicked Land, a people always under the wrath of the Lord. You will see it with your own eyes and say, 'Great is the Lord – even beyond the borders of Israel!' " '

Malachi 1:1–5

Esau and Jacob were the two sons of Isaac, but the names were later given to the two nations that descended from them. Because of their origins the nations were really 'brother nations', but there was never anything but hostility between them. The nation descended from Jacob ended up living in the land of Israel, while those descended from Esau settled in the land of Edom, to the south-east of Israel.

God's love for Israel

Because God's people are disheartened and discouraged after their national defeat and long period in exile, he reminds them of one thing: 'I love you.' And he adds, 'What's more, if you look back through your past you can see the proof of that! Think of all the times you've been wayward, rebellious, and gone off on your own without me. Even so, I've never stopped loving you! I had to shout pretty loud to get you to hear my warnings – your exile wasn't just an accident! But I've brought you back from there, too. I didn't forget about you for one moment; I've never stopped loving you.'

The Edomites, by contrast, had a history of all-out rebellion against God. Israel's history was an up-and-down one, but Edom's seemed to be just down-and-down. To Israel, the thing that had been like a kick in the teeth to them was the way the Edomites acted when Israel was invaded and overpowered by the Babylonians. It seems that the Edomites just stood around watching. They didn't lift a finger to help as they saw their blood-brothers dragged off in chains to captivity, tortured and mutilated. They didn't raise even a squeak of protest on their behalf. In fact, they went one stage worse than doing nothing. The evidence suggests that they cheered on the invaders and gleefully helped them haul the Israelites off to Babylonia.

Israel had been totally devastated by that. It was like a man breaking off all contact with his brother when he hears he's on trial for a robbery; or like a husband walking out on his wife when he discovers she has cancer. Israel felt betrayed, abandoned, hopeless and totally helpless.

Yet God says, 'I know. I know all about that. I saw it all happen. I felt your anguish. I counted all your tears. I want you to know that I really hurt with you during that time. And I'm angry with Edom for their treachery, and will bring them to account for it.'

God's love for his people today

God knows the state of his people today, the church. He knows about all the arguments, divisiveness, in-fighting and the cutting way Christian people behave towards one another. He's seen the lack of power and authority in church life, and the vast numbers of people that leave it each year. He's seen how, in many of our churches, you have to backslide just to fit in! As the people of God together, we're far from God's ideal of what it is to be his people. Even so he says to us, 'I love you. I loved you enough, even knowing of all this failure and error, to send my Son to die for you. And I will not rest until you are holy, the true image of my Son.'

Something remarkable happened when God got involved in Jacob's life. Jacob's name meant 'deceiver' or 'cheat', but God told him all that was to change. And to prove it he gave Jacob a new name, Israel. It was as though God said, 'With my love and guidance, you'll become a different person. It may take time to show, but I'll be changing you from the inside out. I take you for my own; I'm committed to you, and will never let you go.'

Individually too, we are his people. When we're discouraged we need to hear God's words of love and care again. Just as he said to Israel, he says to us, 'I've seen the way your commitment to me goes up and down like a yo-yo. I've seen the way that sometimes you're on fire for me, and sometimes you're freezing cold. But I love you.' He's seen our ups and downs, the good and the bad, and longs to reach out to us with his love and care.

You may be feeling that life's burdens are intolerable right now, and that no one understands what you're going through. That may be true – your situation is unique to you. But God knows what's happening to you, he understands how you feel, and he cares about you more than you can ever grasp. Even if there is fault on your part, that doesn't stop him loving you. He never turns his back on us and says, 'Oh well, then, that's it, isn't it? If you can't do what I say, don't expect to hear from me again!' To prove that he will never say that, he's given us the history of his people, Israel. And that shows us very clearly that God's love is persistent. It never fails. It never stops. It never gives up on us.

Many people have found that in the times of their deepest distress, God gives them a special assurance of his love surrounding and upholding them. A pastor was phoned up one day by a young mum telling him the good news that her second baby had been born. 'God's given me a very special baby,' she said. 'Wonderful!' the pastor replied. 'Yes,' she went on, 'he's only got one hand.' Though the shock that she and her husband felt continued to work its way through, God had taken the edge off their deep disappointment. He had given them a clear assurance that this wasn't a mistake – but that he was trusting them with the special care of this special child.

GOD IS IN CONTROL

It's all very well having a God who loves us, but is he really able to do anything for us? The question that still bothers people today is as old as the hills: 'If God is so loving, why doesn't he do something about the state of the world? Because he's not powerful enough! Or perhaps he is powerful enough, but he doesn't really love us that much to be bothered. No way can God be both loving and powerful!'

Malachi gives a different picture. In his little book of just four chapters he refers to God as 'the Lord of hosts' twenty-five times. It's his favourite name for God: the Lord Almighty, the Lord of the hosts of heaven; Lord of the sun, the moon and all the stars, the planets and everything in the whole of creation. He made it; he's in control of it.

It's great to hear that, but it's sometimes very difficult to believe that God is even interested in what goes on out there in the world, let alone in control of it in some way. We know how he's changed our lives as individuals and how he works with us as a church, but it's harder to read the papers and watch the news on TV and to keep hold of the fact that God is Lord of the whole earth. We're brainwashed by the media into thinking that the ultimate destiny of the planet hangs on the foreign policy of America, or on which third-world countries have nuclear weapons, or on how quickly we can clean up the polluted environment. Yet God's word to Israel was, 'You will see it with your own eyes and say, "Great is the Lord – even beyond the borders of Israel!" ' No politician, army General or terrorist is outside the scope of God's authority. He is Lord of all the earth, in control of events, people and rulers far beyond our circle of knowledge.

God's plans for his people don't stop at personal holiness. They're long-term and global! In Philippians we catch a glimpse of what the goal is to which God is working: 'that at the name of Jesus every knee should bow, in heaven and on earth and under the earth, and every tongue confess that Jesus Christ is Lord, to the glory of God the Father' (Philippians 2:10–11). Such a mighty God has the power to make us holy.

You might have the newest, space-age washing machine, that plays tunes and makes you coffee while you wait for it to do the wash; you might get the best eco-friendly washing powder and fill the machine with carefully filtered water, but if the electricity board has cut off your electricity supply, all those things won't be of much help to you.

God doesn't tell us to be holy – and leave us to flounder around getting nowhere. He gives us his powerful love, forgiveness and grace to see that we really make it.

2

WORSHIP
THAT IS
WORTHY

I remember being taken to Sunday School as a child. One morning I was late, so ran all the way and arrived breathless and dishevelled, one sock up, one down, shirt hanging out and already grubby. I must have looked a real mess. My Sunday School teacher stopped me at the door and, while she tucked my shirt in, she said, 'Stephen, we wouldn't come into the Queen's presence looking like this, would we? We're going into God's house now, so we ought to look our best, shouldn't we?'

I expect many of us had parents who said much the same to us about going to church on Sunday. Getting dressed up in your 'Sunday best' was seen as a mark of respect. But it could also degenerate into an obsession with how you looked. Church life in the 1950s and 1960s especially was obsessed with external appearance. Today if people ask how they should dress for worship, I suggest they come however they feel most comfortable.

But the principle of showing respect for God and his house is one that holds good. Malachi certainly felt that not just the Jewish people, but the priests themselves, had forgotten the majesty of God and had grown dangerously slack in their approach to him:

> ' "A son honours his father, and a servant his master. If I am a father, where is the honour due to me? If I am a master, where is the respect due to me?" says the Lord Almighty. "It is you, O priests, who show contempt for my name.
>
> "But you ask, 'How have we shown contempt for your name?'
>
> "You place defiled food on my altar.
>
> "But you ask, 'How have we defiled you?'
>
> "By saying that the Lord's table is contemptible. When you bring blind animals for sacrifice, is that not wrong? When you sacrifice crippled or diseased animals, is that not wrong? Try offering them to your governor! Would he be pleased with you? Would he accept you?" says the Lord Almighty.

"Now implore God to be gracious to us.
With such offerings from your hands, will he
accept you?" – says the Lord Almighty.'
Malachi 1:6–9

WORSHIP WITH RESPECT

Malachi confronts the priests and people with two pictures from everyday life: parent and child, and master
and servant.

'It's true, isn't it,' he asks, 'that parents are due
respect from their children?' Mum and Dad expect little
Johnny to tidy up the toys when they tell him to, or to
stop bashing his little sister when they tell him that's
not the right way to behave. Teenagers are told to be
home by a certain time of night – trouble starts when
their respect for their parents is not as strong as the
pull to be out with their mates, regardless of the conse-
quences! 'You get annoyed when your children don't
respect you,' says God, 'but you're much worse than
they are! If your children started treating you the same
way you treat me, you'd go off the deep end!'

And then there's the boss. If you invited him and
the Managing Director of your firm home for a meal,
would you serve up last week's left-overs, all mixed up

together? Imagine your boss's reaction if you did! You'd be lucky to have a job the next morning. 'Yet you treat me in just that way,' says God. 'Can't you see how insulting it is?'

The religious laws in the Old Testament stated that people should bring regular sacrifices to the temple, to be offered in penitence for their sin. And the animals brought were to be perfect, without any defect or blemish – no gammy hoof, bad teeth or scruffy hide. But Malachi discovered that the people were going through their herds and flocks, picking out the animals that weren't up to much – the lame, diseased and old ones – the ones they were well rid of anyway, and bringing these instead. 'Try offering those to your governor!' he suggests. 'See what sort of response you get!'

'Try offering those to your boss' is a good guideline to follow. It was probably the thought behind all those parental admonitions: get washed, cut your nails, wear a suit, look solemn, don't talk, walk in and out quietly.' But perhaps we've reacted so far against that sort of approach to church that we've simply fallen off the horse the other side. We've begun to treat worship very casually. We don't often think about our attitude to worship, we're not too bothered about getting there on time, and when we are there we're perfectly happy to chat to people when other things are going on. We pride ourselves on not being hung upon the externals of worship, but what we've put in its place is not the worship of a heart filled with awe and reverence, but the casual commitment of someone who just happens to be here, relaxed and waiting for things to get going.

So how should we approach God in worship?

BRING GOD YOUR BEST

The point Malachi was trying to get across was that it's genuine worship that God wants, worship from the heart – nothing less and nothing else. A substitute for the real thing won't do. Even a pedigree lamb or calf wouldn't have been good enough if the person bringing it did so just for show and not out of genuine love and reverence for God.

> ' "Oh that one of you would shut the temple doors, so that you would not light useless fires on my altar! I am not pleased with you," says the Lord Almighty, "and I will accept no offering from your hands." '   *Malachi 1:10*

A staggering verse! God would actually prefer our churches to close down and be sold off for redevelopment, than have hypocritical, insincere worship going on there. He is not satisfied when we offer him 'rubbish' worship, the worst of our time and possessions rather than our best.

My financial training started very early in life. One important principle I was taught as I grew up was this: 'When you begin to earn, Steve, decide how much you are going to give to God. Then make sure you give it to him first, before you spend anything else, because unless you do, you'll find that the money gets spent on other things and you'll end up giving God just what's left over.' God has the right of access to my money before anyone else does.

The principle doesn't stop with money. God ought to have the best of everything that we have. Often, our lowest time priority is to spend time with God. 'I'll get round to it if I have time.' So we do everything else that needs to be done, and fit God in to the last few moments of the day. Usually, that's our 'tired' time: it's a bit too early to go to bed, but we don't really feel like doing anything much else. So God gets our left-overs.

Plan your giving

If God is going to get the best of our time, abilities and possessions, we'll need to make a definite decision to put him first. That will demand some self discipline; not a very popular thing today:

> ' "Discipline" has become a dirty word in our culture . . . I know I am speaking heresy in many circles, but spontaneity is greatly overvalued. The "spontaneous" person who shrugs off the need for discipline is like the farmer who went out to gather the eggs. As he walked across the farmyard toward the hen house, he noticed the pump was leaking. So he stopped to fix it. It needed a new washer, so he set off to the barn to get one. But on the way he saw that the hay in the hayloft needed straightening, so he went to fetch the pitchfork. Hanging next to the pitchfork was a broom with a broken handle. "I must make a note to myself to buy a new broom handle the next time I get into town," he thought . . .
>
> By now it is clear the farmer is not going to get his eggs gathered, nor is he likely to accomplish anything else he sets out to do. He is utterly, gloriously spontaneous, but he is hardly free. He is, if anything, a prisoner to his unbridled spontaneity.
>
> The fact of the matter is that discipline is the only way to freedom; it is the necessary context for spontaneity.' *John Guest*

Here are some ideas for how to go about planning what you give to God.

• *Make an inventory of your time*. 'When a person gets into the habit of wasting time, he is sure to waste a great deal that does not belong to him.' All the time a Christian has is God's time. Is God getting a good deal on the time he has entrusted to our care? Where does all the time go? Here's one way of finding out:

– Take a sheet of paper and draw two lines across it to divide it into three parts. These parts represent 'morning', 'afternoon' and 'evening'.

– Note down, at the side of each part, the major activities you will be engaged in during the day, such as sleeping, eating, working, playing with the children, housework, study, shopping, travelling, free time, sport . . . or whatever your day involves. Include an 'unaccounted for' line!

– Then, as you go through the day, note down in each part how long you spend on each activity. If you find that a lot of time is 'unaccounted for', do the same exercise the next day, but specify exactly what you are doing for each fifteen-minute period of the day. This will help you to see how your time is being spent.

– When you have done this for a few days, look over the results and ask yourself these questions: Is the way I am spending my time the best way to spend it? Are there things I think are important (perhaps being with the family, visiting an elderly neighbour, spending time in prayer) but that just aren't getting done? Are there things I think unimportant but that I'm spending a lot of time on?

– Now you know where your time is going, plan the next week's activities, dividing each day into 'morning, afternoon and evening' slots, and noting down what you would like to accomplish in each. As someone has said, 'We master our minutes, or we become slaves to them; we use time or it uses us.'

• *Make an inventory of your abilities.* Do the same sort of exercise for your abilities, gifts and areas of interest. The aim is the same: to see what is being underused and what could be better used in God's service. Remember to include all the skills you use at work – often these are invaluable in the church context too.

• *Get the help of friends.* Most of us need other people to help us when we want to stick at something or discipline ourselves. Just think of all the women (and some men) who go to *Weight Watchers*. Are they all stupid? Can't they count calories for themselves? Of course they can! It's just that they're realistic enough to know they need a bit of peer pressure to help them keep up the dieting properly.

Steve Ovett, the runner, once went through a bad patch when he became depressed and fed up with running. So he stopped training. And that might have been the end of his career had not his running partner persisted in dragging him out of bed at six o'clock each morning to go running with him. In time, the old enthusiasm returned – but the skills had been maintained by that crucial partnership.

We all need 'running partners' to help us keep up our Christian commitment. You could covenant with a friend to pray once a week about something specific, instead of watching *Neighbours*. Tell your friend about your resolve to visit that particular person once a month, or your commitment to phone so-and-so regularly over the next eight weeks, and give them permission to keep asking you whether you have!

It is this sort of practical care that we need to take if the responsibilities which God has entrusted to us are going to be discharged well.

• *Be balanced*. Don't be ruled by your diary. It's good to have free time, unplanned and unstructured, when you can relax and do whatever you want to. But remember that spontaneity can be overrated! Try to keep a balance between the two.

CATCH THE BIGGER PICTURE

' "My name will be great among the nations, from the rising to the setting of the sun. In every place incense and pure offerings will be brought to my name, because my name will be great among the nations," says the Lord Almighty.

"But you profane it by saying of the Lord's table, 'It is defiled', and of its food, 'It is contemptible.' And you say, 'What a burden!' and you sniff at it contemptuously," says the Lord Almighty.

"When you bring injured, crippled or diseased animals and offer them as sacrifices, should I accept them from your hands?" says the Lord. "Cursed is the cheat who has an acceptable male in his flock and vows to give it, but then sacrifices a blemished animal to the Lord. For I am a great king," says the Lord Almighty, "and my name is to be feared among the nations." '

Malachi 1:11–14

A growing church

God's great promise to his people is that they are part of something that will ultimately succeed. God is going to speak powerfully to nation after nation, and people all over the world are going to have the chance to respond to God in love and worship.

Today, because of the coming of Jesus, we see this happening in ways Malachi would never have dreamt possible; nor might we have guessed a few decades ago just how fast the Christian church would be growing in some parts of the world. In the city of Seoul in South Korea the church led by Pastor Yonggi Cho now has about half a million members and about twenty thousand housegroups! That's mind-boggling enough. But Paul Yonggi Cho's church isn't the only one in Seoul; there are *lots* of big churches there. There's a Presbyterian Church with 50,000 members, a Baptist Church with 10,000 members, an Episcopal Church with over 25,000 members, and dozens of other churches besides. God is moving in that city. And the same sort of thing is happening in other cities all over the world. There's a revival going on in Rio de Janeiro and in some parts of the city you can go from house to house and find nothing but Christians! The sun of Christianity may appear to be setting over the countries of the West, but it is certainly rising in many countries of the Two-thirds world.

The promise God gave to his people through Malachi, that 'my name will be great among the nations', was already being fulfilled in the rebuilding of the Temple and in the people's recovery from their time of exile. But these things prefigured something far more wonderful. God was assuring his people that they were part of his cosmic, eternal plan. That isn't going to be fulfilled in the next five minutes or next five years, but embraces the whole history of God's people through all ages and to the end of time. The Lord encourages us to look forward to the day when the whole world will know that Jesus Christ is Lord.

You and I may feel pretty insignificant, and our churches in the West may not be very exciting, but God is working among his people. The signs may be quiet, but they are there! I think of the captain of a Boys Brigade Company, and his wife. For many years they laboured and struggled with that group of boys, but now they can see how greatly God has used their work. Some of the church's most committed members and leaders are former members of that Boys Brigade. Or what about three single women who started a Crusader Class over twenty years ago. Now the girls they nurtured, encouraged, prayed over and gave so much of their lives to, are scattered all over the world, working as missionaries, nurses, teachers, and as leaders in the churches in which they have settled.

There's no way we, or the church, will be the losers if we give all that we are and have into his service.

A great God

I spend most of my time preaching 'Fear not' sort of sermons. Jesus was often reassuring his disciples: 'Do not be afraid, little flock, for your Father has been pleased to give you the kingdom' (Luke 12:32). When the disciples were terrified by seeing Jesus walk out to them on the lake in the middle of a storm, he wanted to reassure them: 'It is I; don't be afraid,' he said (John 6:20). And in Revelation, where John has a vision of the risen, exalted Christ, he is paralysed with fear. But Jesus reaches out to him and says, 'Do not be afraid' (Revelation 1:17). And yet, there is a right fear of the Almighty. Because he is so great, God is to be approached with awe and reverence.

In many of our churches, we seem to have lost this godly fear. We need to rediscover it. If we don't, we're going to end up with a false image of God: someone who is our friend and pal, who does things for us if we ask him to – a sort of powerful magician. We will lose the true picture of God as the Almighty Deity whom we are to worship.

In our society, it's hard to keep the right view of God in our sights. Any form of authority tends to be mocked. The authority of the policeman, teachers and the leaders in our communities is challenged in a way it hasn't been before. Subjects are joked about on Saturday evening TV in a way that would have caused a public outcry twenty years ago. The borders of acceptability grow wider, and God himself is well inside them. The danger is that, when we live in an atmosphere that ridicules and belittles all authority, we can easily absorb the same attitude ourselves and bring it with us into our relationship with God.

Check it out for yourself: do you see God as a God to be feared? The God of the Old Testament that the prophets pictured striding the mountains with power so that the whole earth quaked with his voice? Somehow, we don't seem to worship that God any more. Now he is a much more containable God, a God who can be packaged in any way we choose to define him, presented in our own image. He's a God more easily understood; a nice, kinder God; a God at our control.

To worship God in the right way we need to come to him with:

- *Awe*: a sense of wonder, almost fear.
- *Adoration*: our total submission to God. As we admit his greatness, and meditate on his great love for us, we free ourselves to love him. The word 'love' is one that easily becomes cheapened in a decadent society. The

New Testament Christians felt they had to coin a new word for God's love – *agape*. In our day, 'adoration' conveys the depth of our love for God.

● *Reverence*: being aware that we are in the presence of royalty. The way I like to describe reverence is 'worship on tiptoe'. It's thinking carefully about all that you do in worship, all that you say, and listening attentively for God's voice.

A God who cannot be boxed

We cannot tame God, nor mould him to suit the image we prefer. Perhaps we want to keep him in our denominational 'box' – obviously God prefers Anglicans (or Baptists, or Roman Catholics, depending on your own denomination). We need to recognise his living presence in denominations other than our own. He can burst out of our structures, plans and ideas whenever he wants to, and he doesn't need to ask our permission first!

Among evangelicals, the dividing lines today tend to run between different 'theologies' rather than between different denominations. You may be a 'charismatic', but can you see God acting in quiet, unspectacular ways in people's lives? You might be in a traditional, conservative church; are you willing to let God work there in new ways? In our theological arrogance we often want to keep God boxed into one way of relating to us and his church.

Perhaps we feel we can dictate to him how he should act in the life of someone close to us, or how he should change the attitude of the boss at work. If so, we should prepare ourselves for a surprise! He has the complete picture, not just our interpretation of events, and he will act accordingly.

Perhaps we feel despair about the state of the world. If you're an ardent campaigner for cleaner air, the laws on Sunday trading, the abolition of Third-world debts, or anything else that affects our life together on this planet, you will know what it is to be frustrated and discouraged. Even here, God can surprise us with dramatic answers to long years of prayer – take the Berlin wall, for instance! God is great, and he is still in total control of his world. Even the Berlin wall could not hinder the work of his Spirit.

A warning

There's a note of warning at the end of this section: 'Cursed is the cheat' – the person who cheats God out of what is rightfully his. In the Old Testament, when we read of someone being under a 'curse', it doesn't mean that God, in a fit of spite and annoyance, finds a way of getting his own back on a person who disobeys him. A curse was more a statement of a principle: 'If you persist in that course of action, then this is what will inevitably happen to you.' If we deliberately turn our backs on God, then we shall reap the fruit of that disobedience. All that God longs to give us – freedom, joy, love, peace, a worthwhile life – will be beyond our reach.

I see this time and again in people's lives. A lack of trust between marriage partners; strained relationships in the family because one member refuses to forgive and be reconciled; heart attacks brought on by the stress of covering up dishonest dealing at work; AIDS as a result of sexual promiscuity. Society is 'cursed' by these things.

The effects of consistent, prolonged disobedience can be like a curse in a person's life. He has an inner dissatisfaction and lack of fulfilment. The Christian who persists in doing what is wrong – even when he knows it – will not be able to enjoy a stable, peaceful relationship with God. So the hurt and frustration go on, and produce twisted, hurting and distorted people.

We often think we can help people in this situation by changing their circumstances. But what they really need is help to come back to God in repentance. No amount of pastoral care, love or compassion is going to affect the situation of someone living in disobedience to God until that person admits her sin and chooses to release herself from the curse of her own actions.

In his book, *Spiritual Care*, Dietrich Bonhoeffer, a German theologian who died during the Second World War, wrote this:

> 'Disobedience, as well as obedience, has the power to transform a person completely. Through disobedience in a particular decision, one can falsify the whole sequence of right thinking . . .
>
> Disobedience comes in a variety of disguises: as superficial indifference or as the continuous creation of problems; as ascetic rigorism or as sectarianism; as the quest for novelty or as a philosophical restlessness. All that stuff is given a lot of weight pre-eminently to cover a scar in the conscience that lies hidden in the background.'

Know yourself

It's important to know what God's standards are if we are to worship him faithfully. But it is also important to know ourselves. What areas of weakness are there in my life that I need to bring under God's control?

All of us have weak points, areas where we find it really hard to obey God. For many people sexual temptation is the big one. The thoughts come into our minds and we enjoy exploring them – until it dawns on us that they're getting out of control. We shouldn't have let them in in the first place, let alone encourage them to stay. If this is an area of weakness for you, you will always need to be on your guard against giving sexual temptation a foothold in your mind. Displace it by encouraging right thoughts and loyalties to grow there instead: remember your pledge of loyalty to your husband or wife; turn your thoughts to the Lord of your life who died to make you his own, and let love for him fill your mind.

Others of us are workaholics – always working and not giving the time we should to our families, to God in prayer, to relaxing and just being human. It's a constant struggle to disentangle ourselves from the demands of work. If you are naturally conscientious, you will always find it hard to keep work inside its fences. The secret is to want God's good gifts even more! To want to spend time with him, to enjoy the kids, to discover the world he's put us in.

Others of us are basically lazy and have to be kick-started into doing anything at all. We can be really sure

God is prompting us to invite our next door neighbour to church, or to sit down and plan the family holiday, but somehow we just don't get round to it. It is crucial to admit this tendency to ourselves, and to plan ways to fight against it. Get the help of a friend – someone with whom you can share your plans and who will keep asking whether you've put them into practice yet!

William Temple defined worship as 'bringing all that we know of ourselves to all that we know of God.' That means the weak patches of our characters as well as the good bits. Once we allow God's holiness and greatness to probe every area of our lives, he can begin to heal and restore them, change our perspective and our priorities, and help us to worship him with the respect and love he is due.

3

A

FAITHFUL

REPRESENTATIVE

John Stott, an Anglican minister well known for his writing and teaching, was once asked a question about his devotional life. 'When you get down on your knees and pray to God, how do you feel about your relationship with him? What happens to you?' He answered, 'When I kneel and close my eyes, it's like finding myself against a brick wall. For quite some time as I pray and read the Bible, I feel as if I'm blindly groping my way along this wall, desperately trying to find some way into God's presence. For a while, it's just terrible! I feel as if I'm just going through the motions of prayer. But suddenly I get to a point, after a while of praying and praising and reading the Scriptures, where it's as though my hand comes on the door handle of a huge door; it swings open in front of me and I burst through into a glorious sunshine beyond. At that point, I know I'm in the presence of God.'

THE DOOR INTO GOD'S PRESENCE

John Stott says that it takes time to find the door into God's presence, and that the key to unlock it is the key of fixing his mind, will and spirit on the one goal of hearing God. It means getting to the point of saying, 'Lord, I want to hear from you, and I'm now ready to receive whatever you have to say.' Stott adds that until he does reach that point everything else he says is just empty words because he's not really ready to accept what God wants to say to him.

We can read our Bibles and pray every day, hear the word of God expounded each week, go to Christian conferences every year and hear more of God's word taught there. But we can still hold ourselves back from God – not letting him into our emotions, spirits, minds and wills for him to change them. Malachi had this to say to some people who must have known God's word

inside out – the priests – yet their spirits were not
willing to come under its authority:

' "And now this admonition is for you, O
priests. If you do not listen, and if you do not
set your heart to honour my name," says the
Lord Almighty, "I will send a curse upon you,
and I will curse your blessings. Yes, I have
already cursed them, because you have not set
your heart to honour me.

"Because of you I will rebuke your descendants; I will spread on your faces the offal from
your festival sacrifices, and you will be carried
off with it. And you will know that I have sent
you this admonition so that my covenant with
Levi may continue," says the Lord Almighty.

"My covenant was with him, a covenant of
life and peace, and I gave them to him; this called
for reverence and he revered me and stood in
awe of my name. True instruction was in his
mouth and nothing false was found on his lips.
He walked with me in peace and uprightness,
and turned many from sin.

"For the lips of a priest ought to preserve
knowledge, and from his mouth men should seek
instruction – because he is the messenger of the
Lord Almighty. But you have turned from the
way and by your teaching have caused many to
stumble; you have violated the covenant with
Levi," says the Lord Almighty. "So I have caused
you to be despised and humiliated before all the
people, because you have not followed my ways

but have shown partiality in matters of the law." '   *Malachi 2:1–9*

The admonition that Malachi brings to the priests is a devastating one. There is no cruder, more violent language against priests and their shallow religiosity anywhere in the minor prophets. He takes them by the scruff of the neck, shakes them up and says, 'There's absolutely no integrity about the way you carry out your duties as priests! You say all the right words and do all the right things outwardly, but in your hearts you despise me and couldn't care less about my people!'

PRIESTS OF THE NEW COVENANT

The tabloids love it when they can get hold of a story of a 'naughty vicar' and splash the sordid details all over their front pages. People still feel particularly cheated when someone they have trusted betrays that trust or takes advantage of their position of responsibility. Recently, the media spotlight has not been so much on church ministers as on parents and teachers who abuse the trust of the children in their care. Many people have felt the same sort of outrage and cynicism over the misuse of the pension funds held by Robert Maxwell.

This sort of hypocrisy sickens us: people posing as good, upright and trustworthy, while all the time fleecing those who take them at their word. So when we see their come-uppance, we're glad. 'Great! They're getting the hammering they deserve! Isn't it good that they're being criticised – those "holy men"?'

It's easy to point the finger. But we are the priests of the new covenant. All who live this side of the cross, by faith in Christ, are called to pray for others, and to set an example of holy living. Malachi's words to the priests of his day don't apply just to those 'in holy orders' but to all who call themselves Christians.

UNITY OF WORD AND ACTION

Part of a prayer of confession in a recent service during the Week of Prayer for Christian Unity, went like this:

> 'We acknowledge that in many ways
>   our lives lack unity.
> Between the ideals and the pressures
>   there is compromise.
> Between the dreams and the realities
>   there are frustrations.

Between the belief and the expression
    there is misunderstanding and conflict.
And so we turn to you to unite us.

Lord, to whom else could we go?
    You alone have the words of eternal life.
As we centre our lives on you,
    melt our divisions and make us one.'

Malachi takes the same idea of a divided people, but applies it to the life of the individual. It's not just relationships with others that are fragmented and cold, but within ourselves there are divided loyalties, different aims and desires, all pulling us in different directions.

I have known dozens of Christians who made a commitment to Christ many years ago and who now read their Bibles, pray, and think their spiritual act is together. But in reality they have never come to the point of saying, 'God, I really will do what you tell me to do. I will bring my life in line with what your word says: in what I think, in what I desire, in what I do.'

Malachi's plea is for integrity: full integration of the body, mind, will and emotions in God's service. Integrity means 'oneness': being the same in what we do as in what we say. The things we say on Sunday at church are to be worked out in the way we behave on Monday at work.

Suppose you were talking with a Christian friend at work about what you were doing on Sunday. Then a non-Christian colleague comes along and joins in the conversation. I guess the topic would change very quickly! Of course, it may have to; the non-Christian may not understand a word of what we're on about. But often it's easier to be one sort of person with our Christian friends, and another with our non-Christian friends – a person we think will be more acceptable to them.

One of the tragedies affecting the Renewal movement in this country is that some people have simply taken on the language of renewal without its reality. In the last twenty years we have learnt to talk about the Holy Spirit; to say, 'Yes, Holy Spirit, come and fill my life,' but for many of us, that's as far as it has gone. Our vocabulary has changed, but the holiness of our lives hasn't. Let's not just talk about being filled with the Holy Spirit, but *be* filled with him. Let us not just talk about how important it is to be holy, but *be* holy as the people of God.

When I was an impressionable young teenager I was made paranoid about holiness of life by a speaker at a youth conference. He read two verses from Luke's Gospel, which say: 'There is nothing concealed that will not be disclosed, or hidden that will not be made known. What you have said in the dark will be heard in the daylight, and what you have whispered in the inner rooms will be proclaimed from the roofs' (Luke 12:2–3).

Then he looked round at this crowd of insecure, guilt-ridden young Christians and said, 'One day, everything you have ever done that was wrong is going to be shouted from the roof tops!' We were terrified! 'Oh no!' I groaned; 'my parents will find out!'

Now I realise that the speaker's interpretation of those verses was completely wrong. They were actually given by Jesus to his disciples as a word of encouragement and comfort as they put up with the taunts and ridicule of the powerful Pharisees. 'Don't worry,' Jesus says, 'You may have to watch what you say about me now, but the day is coming when you'll be able to shout the gospel from the roof tops: it won't be suppressed any more.'

I believe far more harm than good came out of that speaker's misinterpretation of those verses. Many young people suffered a sort of holy paranoia for years after. We were kept in line spiritually through sheer stark fear that one day everyone would know exactly what we'd been up to and what we'd said and done. The prospect still haunts me! All the things I shouted and screamed at the kids last night in order to get them ready for bed; the snide thing I said to my wife when she burnt the dinner – all that on a big screen in front of the congregation in five minutes' time for everyone to see!

But if he can't tell us anything about what those verses in Luke mean, that youth speaker can tell us something about the nature of integrity. Our lives are to be more and more transparent; less and less clouded by pretence.

SETTING THE PACE

Malachi lived in a confusing time. It was difficult to know for sure what was right and what was wrong. The whole of their society was only just emerging from total devastation; surely it was natural that the leaders and the people didn't really know what God expected of them? The lives of the Jewish people were messy and chaotic, through circumstances beyond their control.

There's a difference between an outwardly chaotic life and an inwardly chaotic one. You may be going through the most messy of circumstances. Perhaps a house move, job change, something intensely unsettling like the break up of a relationship. The lives of the

Jewish people were messy and chaotic in this sense: their broken-down buildings had to be rebuilt and their social structures had to be put back on a stable footing. Yet even though the Temple had been rebuilt, they let their inner spiritual lives stay in a mess. The priests were going through all the right motions but, underneath, they couldn't care less about the God they were supposed to be doing it all for.

The hypocrisy of the Jewish leaders spread to the rest of the people like an infectious disease: 'You have turned from the way and by your teaching have caused many to stumble' (Malachi 2:8). If you are in a leadership position – whether on the shop floor, in the office or in church life – remember that the people you lead will grow to absorb and reflect your own way of thinking and behaving. If they think you're hypocritical and insincere, they'll be wary of you and become devious in the way they relate to you and one another. If you always know best and won't listen to any other opinions, the people in your care will soon see it's no use trying to talk about anything with you. So they'll either grow apathetic, go somewhere else, or stay and become a pain in the neck! In church life, it's a rare person who can live consistently beyond the low spiritual standards of his or her spiritual leaders.

I feel the pain of any challenge to my integrity. And that's because the accusation is often right – at least in part. None of us are completely whole people, wholly integrated. All our lives we'll be doing God's work from mixed motives, without total commitment, with plenty of selfishness and pride mixed in. But Malachi reminds me that wilful and deliberate internal disunity is a disease that will gradually destroy my spiritual health and, as a leader, will put in jeopardy the spiritual health of the people in my care.

LIVES THAT BLESS OTHERS

When the reviews of Julia Roberts' performance in *Pretty Woman* dripped with her praises, she made a supersonic bound forward in her film career. But suppose a member of the Cabinet did something that was warmly praised by his rival in the Opposition; that praise would be more like a millstone round his neck! Receiving praise from the wrong people can mean the kiss of death to a person's hopes and plans!

Malachi warns the priests that, in the same way, their blessings on the people will be worse than useless. 'I will curse your blessings,' God tells them. 'Yes, I have already cursed them, because you have not set your heart to honour me' (Malachi 2:2). In blessing the people, the priests were saying, 'Lord, please give them all the things you've given me.' From now on, says God, that will be asking for trouble in a big way! Someone blessed by one of those priests could count on a future as secure and blessed as the Pope's would be if he were hailed by 'Teflon Don', the godfather of the mafia, as a close friend and confidant!

As priests of the new covenant, how can we make sure our lives are a blessing to others and not a curse?

• *Bless by your words.* There are other priestly ways of blessing people than saying, 'God bless you!' As a priest of the new covenant, make sure that all you say is a true reflection of the mind of God. Hasty, bitter and angry words can cut far more deeply than we think they can, and can leave a person wounded for years. By contrast, God deals with us gently and kindly. He encourages us and builds us up, helping us to grow strong in those areas where we are weak. The cumulative effect of his words to us is blessing. Our words also should encourage and affirm others.

• *Bless by your actions.* You don't need to raise your arms over a congregation, or make the sign of the cross, to give people a priestly blessing! We bless others by doing kind things for them, sacrificing our time and energy on their behalf.

• *Bless consistently.* The test of a good pastor or preacher is consistency. Can he care for his flock, or preach consistently, no matter how he's feeling? The same goes for a priest. In whatever situation we're in we should be looking for ways to bring blessing to others. Keep the question in the forefront of your mind: 'How can I bless the people I meet today?' That applies especially to our families. We all hear stories of pastors or priests who bless their congregations on a Sunday morning, then go home and are miserable, domineering or sulky with their families. A priest of the new covenant should always be asking, 'how can I be a blessing today to my wife/husband, children, neighbour?'

LIVES THAT MIRROR GOD'S PURITY

The priests that Malachi saw prided themselves on their special position. They expected people to treat them with respect and receive with gratefulness any kind words they might utter. But Malachi challenged all that. 'You think that all you touch turns to gold? In fact, all you touch is doomed to destruction. You don't purify people by being with them, you defile them in God's sight!'

> ' "Because of you I will rebuke your descendants; I will spread on your faces the offal from your festival sacrifices, and you will be carried off with it." '
> *Malachi 2:3*

When the priests offered a sacrifice, they were to remove all the animal's innards or offal, because it was considered to be 'unclean', offensive to God. Then the innards were taken right outside the inhabited area of town and dumped in the rubbish pit. 'Yet,' says God, 'you might as well be offering me nothing but offal on those sacrifices. Everything you do is as horrible, offensive and loathsome as the most unclean thing you could offer me. That's what I think of your spiritual leadership, of your lack of integrity. It stinks! It's unclean! You think you're getting rid of the ceremonial uncleanness by taking away the innards and burning them, but you're not, because the uncleanness is inside you.' Nowhere in the Old Testament is there another such damning condemnation of empty religiosity.

In Malachi's day the Jewish people boasted that

God had given his Law to *them*, not to anyone else, and that their God was greater than anyone else's. But the nations around simply looked and scoffed and said, 'Then why aren't you *keeping* his Law, especially if he's such a great and powerful God?'

People outside the church expect to find integrity inside it. They're always hearing the church talk about morals, ethical standards and values, so when they look inside they expect to see men and women who say what they mean and mean what they say. But if they look hard, they'll probably find Christians cheating on their Income Tax, or leading immoral sexual lives and generally seeming no different from anyone else. As long as there is a gap between what we profess and what we do, the world will say, 'So what?' to our faith. Those outside the church can often spot our lack of integrity more quickly than our Christian friends can. We can fool our friends because they already trust us. Someone who doesn't have any reason for trusting us needs to have proof of our integrity before he will.

In a survey I conducted a few years ago to find out the questions and feelings non-Christians had about Christians and the church, the comment I heard most often was: 'Well I don't want to be a Christian; I know one and his behaviour is lousy!' Hypocrisy is the number one problem for non-Christians; a lack of integrity in the lives of God's people.

Every so often we need to give ourselves a spiritual MOT. Here are some things to check over:

• *Is everything above board*? We need to live truthful lives, not just in what we say, but in how we justify our actions. 'It'll be all right if I take just a few sheets of paper from the office without paying; after all, I worked through part of my lunch hour today.' Or, 'I might as well stay at a five star hotel on this business trip; if I didn't, and claimed for the expense anyway, the firm would pay up!' Self-justification is very deceptive. There is often more than one way of looking at a situation. Many of the dilemmas we find ourselves in are not easy to untangle, and the right way to act is not always clear. But we should hear warning bells when we realise we're trying to justify our actions to ourselves. The chances are that they're not entirely above board.

• *Develop a guilty conscience.* Two men ran a tailoring business. One day their young assistant was left in charge of the shop while one partner was out and the other worked in the back room. A wealthy lady came in to collect a new blouse she had ordered. After she had paid for it and gone, the young assistant suddenly realised she'd paid for her £49.99 blouse with a £100 note instead of a £50 note – but he'd only given her change for £50.

Thinking he should run after her and hand over the rest of her change, he dashed first into the back room and said to his boss: 'Look! That lady gave me £100 note, but I only gave her change for £50! What should I do?' His boss thought for a while then said, 'Well, the moral issue is a straightforward one: do I tell my partner, or do the two of us share the extra between ourselves?'

Whose moral standards are we following – the Bible's or those of the people with whom we live day by day? Like a set of bad scales, our conscience can gradually get inaccurate and needs to be readjusted along biblical lines.

• *How do I react when people ask probing questions?* Suppose your house group leader announced that she was going to tail you for a week, coming to work with you each day and wandering about in your house in the evenings. Would there be things you wanted to hide from her? Things you'd rather she didn't know about? When people start getting close to us, either by being around or by asking probing questions, our reactions may tell us something about the integrity of our lifestyle. If we quickly feel 'got at' it may be a sign of an uneasy conscience.

A FAITHFUL REPRESENTATIVE

In the middle of the report of the priest's base behaviour, Malachi sets a gem: a lovely description of the life of a man or woman of God, when that life faithfully reflects God's character.

> ' "Levi . . . revered me and stood in awe of my name. True instruction was in his mouth and nothing false was found on his lips. He walked with me in peace and uprightness, and turned many from sin." ' *Malachi 2:5–6*

I guess we'd all like to have that epitaph on our tomb stones! Levi was one of the sons of Jacob, and it was his male descendants who were called by God to be priests for the rest of the people of Israel. The description Malachi gives here is of a typical Levite early on in Israel's history, when they were still taking their priestly task seriously. It shows us a person who tells the truth about the things of God, who doesn't lie or cheat, manipulate or deceive. He is transparently honest and open, and lives life in company with God. Any who are like him are his true descendants.

All Christian believers are called to be priests in the work of Christ, offering spiritual worship and sacrifices of praise and obedience (see 1 Peter 2:4–12). We are the contemporary descendants of Levi, and our lives should match the description given of him.

The picture is of someone who gently but firmly gets involved in the life of the people around and, among other things, 'turns many from sin'. A recent survey about muggings on the streets of New York revealed that nine muggings out of ten happen while other people looked on and did nothing about it. And an article in *The Times* in January 1992, headlined '750 police attacked in ten days', read:

> 'The public should be more willing to help police who are attacked, the Association of Chief Police Officers said yesterday as it released figures showing that nearly 750 officers were attacked over Christmas and the new year . . .
>
> The association, which represents chief constables, said: "We don't want to put anyone at risk but all too often many officers report that when they are struggling with an offender in the street, members of the public just stand there and look on when some modest gesture of physical support might be all that is needed." '

We don't want to get involved. 'That's somebody else's problem.' 'He's paid to do that.' 'I may get dragged into the whole business.' We are becoming increasingly isolated from one another in society, running from the safety of our nuclear-family houses to the security of the office, and back again, talking to as few people in between as possible. All kinds of sociological pressures push us into this way of living.

It's so easy to drink in the spirit of the age. When we see the neighbour's son getting increasingly involved in some harmful activity, or hear one neighbour's bitchy comments about another, we pray for them, of course. But we also prefer to let them go their own way than to take the risky step of 'interfering'. And we justify that by telling ourselves, 'They don't want me to get involved; they'll think I'm just a nosey busybody.'

The godly priest is defined as one who does get involved; not in a pushy way, but by being bothered about how others behave, and drawing them back from the brink of wrong with love and compassion.

Getting involved without getting people's backs up

When we are concerned about someone, how can we get involved without getting their backs up? Here are some suggestions:

• Speak with genuine humility. Don't assume you are speaking with the voice of God; it is possible that your perception of the situation might be wrong! An arrogant approach will very quickly alienate people but a gentle, humble approach may help to draw them out: 'I don't want to interfere but it seems to me that . . .' 'Please tell me if my perception is all wrong, but it appears to me that . . .'

• Write to the person concerned. That gives them more time to weigh up what you are saying, and gives you more time to choose your words carefully. You can also be more subtle, simply hinting at an area where you think there may be problems. Perhaps a couple seem to be drifting apart; you could broach it by writing something like: 'If John's long hours at work ever are a problem, I'd be happy to do what I can . . .' Open up the possibility for communication.

• Invite the person round for coffee, so that you create a 'natural' time for talking.

• Cultivate your friendships deliberately, both inside and outside the church. Get to know people increasingly well, and don't stay content with superficial levels of friendship.

• Let people know that the church as a whole is a place of refuge and resource. *You* might not be the person your next door neighbour wants to unburden herself to, but she may be prepared to find someone else at church with whom she'll feel happier to do so.

• Live an approachable lifestyle. Take the long way round to the shops if it means you're likely to see more people to speak to. Allow extra time for those 'chance' conversations in Sainsburys or Tescos. Be around, be visible. Of course, it's not always possible to live like this; the pressures of work don't allow it. In that case, schedule into your diary planned times of 'slack', when you can be available to others without feeling guilty about the work that's not getting done.

• If your church has just one service on a Sunday, use the rest of the day constructively to build up friendships and get to know your neighbours. Invite them round for the evening, or invite out for the afternoon that new couple from church. Our time and our homes are gifts from God to use in building up his kingdom. Let's use them!

4

COMMITMENT
IN PERSONAL
RELATIONSHIPS

Jewish tradition would have us believe that the problem of unfaithfulness in marriage is one that has plagued us from the dawn of time. Whenever Adam was late back home, the story goes, Eve counted his ribs to make sure God hadn't made another woman out of them!

Malachi, too, speaks of marriage and faithfulness in the context of creation – the creation of the people of Israel:

> 'Have we not all one Father? Did not one God create us? Why do we profane the covenant of our fathers by breaking faith with one another? Judah has broken faith. A detestable thing

has been committed in Israel and in Jerusalem: Judah has desecrated the sanctuary the Lord loves, by marrying the daughter of a foreign god. As for the man who does this, whoever he may be, may the Lord cut him off from the tents of Jacob – even though he brings offerings to the Lord Almighty.'   *Malachi 2:10–12*

Malachi is confronting the people with the fact that they have broken their covenant of commitment to him. God sees our decision to follow him and commit ourselves to him as being as binding and exclusive as a marriage covenant. And when we turn away from that commitment, it is as painful to him as adultery. He says that the Israelites, who once faithfully pledged themselves to him as their only God, have forgotten all about him and are taken up instead with 'the daughter of a foreign god.' All their time, concern and interests are directed towards everything but God.

MARRIED TO CHRIST

In the New Testament, Paul speaks of Christians being the bride of Christ (Ephesians 5:25–27). When you became a Christian, you gave your life to Christ. He came to live inside you and the two of you became one. The divine life of God joined itself with your spirit, and a sort of supernatural oneness took place. God came to live inside you – the new, number one relationship in your life. It is a unique relationship between God and you. An abbot called Symeon, who lived in the tenth century, described the wonder of it like this:

'He was suddenly completely there,
united with me in an ineffable manner,
joined to me in an unspeakable way
and immersed in me without mixing
as the fire melds one with the iron,
and the light with the crystal.
And he made me as though I were all fire.
And he showed me myself as light
and I became that which before I saw
and I had contemplated only from afar.
I do not know how to express to you
the paradox of this manner.
For I was unable to know
and I still now do not know
how he entered, how he united himself with me . . .
Nevertheless, having become one being,
I and he to whom he was united,
how shall I call myself?
God, having two natures, is one person;
he has made me a double being.'

When we live as if God is just one among many relationships that we have, or even act as if he's not there at all, we're living a divorce; we're divorcing God. Some of us divorce him from our daily lives, not thinking of him from one week to the next. Some of us divorce him from our sexual lives – not allowing him any say in what happens there. Or perhaps we divorce him from our moral and ethical life – what goes on at work, for instance. Some of us divorce him from everything apart from the religious bit. We keep him wrapped up in a box and stick a label on it that says: 'For Sunday morning, Sunday night and house-group night only. Do not let out at any other time!' And we'll only release God into our lives on those occasions. That's like keeping your spouse locked up; perhaps allowing him or her to use the bathroom and the bedroom, but not any other room in the house.

God calls us back to a full marriage relationship with himself, to be completely and utterly faithful to him. Only then, when God is fully involved in every aspect of our life, will our behaviour as Christians be filled with integrity.

It's easy to think that ministers, pastors and other people in full-time Christian work don't have this problem. After all, they spend all their time reading the Bible or praying, preaching or counselling, don't they? But even for those of us in that sort of work, our marriage to Christ has to be maintained. Unless I *invite* God into every situation, he won't be there, despite the fact that I may be going through the religious exercises. I can counsel someone and leave God completely out of it by not inviting his Spirit and his word to cast light on the problem. I can even read the Bible without inviting God to speak with me through it. You might find me at nine o'clock on a Sunday morning, frantically leafing through Malachi chapter 2 and saying, 'Lord, you must have *something* to say out of this!' That's just using God to get a sermon or talk; studying the Bible for its own sake, rather than to hear what God has to say to me.

Perhaps you teach a class at school, work in a factory or office, travel a lot in the car or deal with people – whatever your situation, if God is divorced from it there will be a lack of integrity in your life. You are married to Christ. So, day by day, invite him into every aspect of your life, so that he becomes fully part of it.

MARRIAGE WITHIN THE CONTEXT OF FAITH

The Jews had done something which brought real problems in their relationship with God. Many of them had married people from another culture and race. Now that in itself is not a problem. It can be very enriching. The Bible gives examples of good, God-honouring marriages between people of different races and cultures. The problem with the marriages that Malachi saw as he looked around was that the Jews had married people who had no commitment to God. Those people had brought their own 'gods' into the marriage. They had different priorities and moral standards, and certainly didn't try to live their lives according to what God wanted.

That still happens today. A young Christian woman falls in love with a nice, kind, good-looking guy – who's not a Christian. So what? Does it matter? As long as he's happy for her to carry on going to church, isn't it all right? And anyway, won't she be able to have a good influence on him, and bring him to faith in Christ, too?

But isn't it a bit underhand to marry someone hoping to convert him or her? We feel hypocritical if we invite someone to an evangelistic service at church without first telling them what's going to happen. It doesn't seem any better to marry someone with the aim of converting him after!

Many young Christian women, feeling the pressure to get married, have gone ahead with marriage to a non-Christian. The years that follow are not always as happy as they had hoped. Here is a letter written by one such woman to a younger girl in her church:

'I watched you tonight; I wished for an opportunity to talk with you. I watched your beautiful face as you sang and worshipped. You reminded me of myself seven years ago. And then, after church, I watched you as you got into that car with a boy who does not know God. Oh yes, he was at church tonight. He even went to the altar and shed a few tears. I am sure you would not accept the idea that for him this is just a means to an end.

Seven years ago I was in your shoes. I had known God since my early teens, and had grown up under God-anointed preaching and teaching. I didn't lack boyfriends or dates, as is so often the case with Christian girls in churches where the girls outnumber the boys. Some very consecrated, wonderful young men came my way. But Satan, who watches diligently and waits patiently to ensnare a soul, saw me one day as I was lukewarm. Oh, I was still going to church and doing all the right things outwardly. But I had never really had that special moment with God when his will and mine were made one.

I met him at work. And before long, without anyone else knowing it, I felt I couldn't live without him. He knew about genuine Christianity, and when he went to church with me, he went to the altar and cried.

And so I married him, while my family and those who loved me wept and agonised.

It was just six months after, that I realised my soul was in danger and that I needed a special touch from God. I prayed through, and got a grip on God. Then the battle began. No, he wasn't going to church any more. I can count on my fingers the number of times he's been during the last seven years. Before I married him, the thought of living without him was unbearable. 'How lonely I would be!' I thought. But now I know what real loneliness is, and I'd like to tell you about it.

Loneliness is receiving a blessing from God and going home to a man you can't share it with. He isn't interested; he's watching television. Loneliness is going to a church social alone and watching the young couples enjoy God's blessings together. You can go alone or stay at home alone; he has other interests.

Loneliness is feeling the urgency of Christ's coming and knowing the one you love most on earth is not ready, and shows no signs of caring.

Loneliness is seeing two children born and knowing that if your influence is to outweigh his it will be a miracle.

Loneliness is going to a General Conference and seeing young couples everywhere who are truly one and dedicated to God's work. And there goes the young man who loved you once and wanted to marry you. He's preaching the gospel now, and has never married. Oh, God! Help me! I mustn't think of it.

Loneliness is lying awake struggling with the suspicion that he's unfaithful. Then comes the unbelievable pain of knowing for sure. He doesn't care if I know. She even calls me on the 'phone. After a time, he makes an effort to break it off. I vow to do everything humanly possible to keep this marriage together. I will love him more and pray for him more. Seven years of my life are involved in this. There's a little girl and a little boy!

Loneliness is now. My children and I will go home to a dark, empty apartment that will be my home till the lawyer says it's all over. I, who have always been afraid to stay alone, now welcome the peace and solitude. As I look in the mirror I see that seven years haven't changed my face so much. But inside I am old, and something that was alive once and was beautiful is now dead.

Of course, this is not an unusual story. The remarkable thing about it is that I am still living for God. I am thankful for my family and their prayers of intercession for me!

Oh, I am praying for you, Christian girl. Please believe me when I tell you that no matter how wonderful he is – you cannot build a happy life upon disobedience to God's word. You see, no matter what the future holds for me, I have missed his perfect will for my life. I will never stop paying for breaking a commandment of God's.

Don't let it happen to you.'

The Bible is clear in its teaching on marriage between Christians and non-Christians:

> 'Do not be yoked together with unbelievers. For what do righteousness and wickedness have in common? Or what fellowship can light have with darkness? What harmony is there between Christ and Belial? What does a believer have in common with an unbeliever? What agreement is there between the temple of God and idols? For we are the temple of the living God.'
>
> *2 Corinthians 6: 14–16*

Marriage is the most intimate relationship anyone can have with another person – the physical relationship combined with a lifelong commitment to that person. So the Bible teaches that a Christian's marriage partner must also be someone in whom Christ lives, and who puts Christ first.

This is a principle with an incredible cost, but it is part of the total cost of discipleship. For young women in particular, who in most areas of the UK still outnumber the men in our churches, the cost is very great. It is for all of us, and especially those in leadership in churches, to make sure that church is a place where singles are welcomed as single people, and helped to take a full part in church life. Churches can sometimes feel as if they're designed only for couples or children, making single people feel different and excluded.

If you are a single Christian, and feel the pull of marriage to a non-Christian, what can you do to help yourself?

• Tell God about it, and say exactly how you feel. The first need is to be totally frank with yourself and him about the temptations you struggle with and the fears you face. When we are honest with God, we open the door for him to get to work in that situation.

• Share your feelings with a mature Christian of your own sex, whom you trust and get on well with. Ask him or her to support you in sticking to what you know to be right. It will need to be someone who will pray for you and with you regularly – try to meet with him or her once a week for a short time of chat and prayer together. Perhaps you could widen the focus of your prayers together to include others in similar situations or going through other struggles.

• Allow Christ to take first priority in your life. You will need to be determined that he alone is going to rule in your life, even above your own wishes, desires and fears.

- Find out where the single Christians meet. If there isn't any one place or group, suggest to your church leaders that you start one.
- Remember that your choices in this area of life don't affect just you. You can guarantee that the younger girls and guys in the church will be watching your every move with avid interest! That can be intensely annoying, but it does mean that, whether you like it or not, you are being a role model for them. You are giving them a living demonstration, by what you do, of what it means to be a Christian.

Remember that God wants the best for you. The Lord who gave up his life for you isn't going to stand idly by while you suffer torments. Don't lose faith that he has good plans for your life.

What if you are already in the difficult position of being married to someone who is not a Christian, and perhaps not at all sympathetic to your faith either? Your commitment to him (and it usually is 'him') is precious, and something God can use for his good. So:

- Continue to be committed to him. The fact that he's not a Christian doesn't give you the right to walk out on him.

• Love him. When this is hard, ask for God's love to fill you. Ask to be able to see him in the light of God's great love for him.

• Pray for him. And encourage a few close Christian friends to pray for him, too, without making him feel the victim of a Christian campaign! It may take many years for him to come to know and love the Lord Jesus, so stick at it. God will honour your resolution.

FAITHFULNESS WITHIN MARRIAGE

All through this chapter of Malachi, the ideas of faithfulness to God and faithfulness to other people are intertwined. It seems you cannot have one without the other:

> 'Another thing you do: You flood the Lord's altar with tears. You weep and wail because he no longer pays attention to your offerings or accepts them with pleasure from your hands. You ask, "Why?" It is because the Lord is acting as the witness between you and the wife of your youth, because you have broken faith with her, though she is your partner, the wife of your marriage covenant.
>
> Has not the Lord made them one? In flesh

and spirit they are his. And why one? Because
he was seeking godly offspring. So guard yourself
in your spirit, and do not break faith with the
wife of your youth.

"I hate divorce," says the Lord God of
Israel, "and I hate a man's covering himself with
violence as well as with his garment," says the
Lord Almighty.

So guard yourself in your spirit, and do not
break faith.'   *Malachi 2: 13–16*

In Malachi's day Jewish men were guilty of divorcing
their wives very casually and easily. Women, of course,
were rarely in a position to divorce their husbands in
that society. Some Rabbis taught that if a woman put
too much salt on her husband's lunch, he could divorce
her. I can't see many marriages lasting longer than the
honeymoon on that basis! One Rabbi claimed that, 'If
you see a woman who pleases your eye more, you
may divorce your first wife.' But others like Malachi
disagreed and said that attitude was a complete denial
of what God taught in his law. 'The wife of your youth
was given to you in covenant by God,' they said. 'That
covenant must not be broken.'

In Matthew's Gospel, Jesus said that divorce could
be allowed on one ground only, something he called
'uncleanness' or 'unchastity'. But it's very hard to know

exactly what he meant by the term he used. In any case, he taught that divorce is the very last resort, and insisted strongly that it was not what God wanted (Matthew 5: 31–32).

'I hate divorce,' says God. The word is very strong – God loathes and detests divorce. But *he does not hate people who have been divorced*. It's vital to get that clear. If you have suffered the pain of divorce, you'll understand why God hates it. He hates to see people in pain. He knows the dislocation it brings to the human psyche. He knows all about the social problems it brings when a person to whom you have been committed is wrenched away from you.

God sees the social fabric of society being torn to shreds. Teachers today can count on the fingers of one hand the number of children in their classes who still live with both natural parents. And God understands the terrible loneliness of having to raise children on your own. He knows the anguish and hell of having someone you trusted and gave your life to, no longer on the scene. It's worse than losing a limb. The agony of divorce rests in your soul and grips you to the point of tears, and you feel so lost and alone in a hostile world. That's why God hates divorce.

If you have been through a divorce or separation,

or are going through it now, God wants you to know that he hates what has happened to you with an almighty, divine hatred. *But he doesn't hate you one little bit.* When Jesus started his ministry, he quoted the prophet Isaiah, who spoke powerfully about God's desire to rebuild lives that have been broken and ruined, like cities that have been attacked and had their walls broken to pieces:

'The Spirit of the Sovereign Lord is on me,
    because the Lord has anointed me
    to preach good news to the poor.
He has sent me to bind up the broken-hearted,
    to proclaim freedom for the captives,
    and release from darkness for the prisoners,
to proclaim the year of the Lord's favour
    and the day of vengeance of our God,
to comfort all who mourn,
    and provide for those who grieve in Zion –
to bestow on them a crown of beauty
    instead of ashes,
the oil of gladness
    instead of mourning,
and a garment of praise
    instead of a spirit of despair.
They will be called oaks of righteousness,
    a planting of the Lord
    for the display of his splendour.
They will rebuild the ancient ruins
    and restore the places long devastated.'
Isaiah 61: 1–4

God longs to rebuild and restore those who have been devastated through divorce. That couldn't be clearer. And there are ways we can help that process:

● Have confidence in God. He doesn't reject you, and divorce isn't the unforgiveable sin. God takes us from where we are – not from where we ought to be – and leads us on into the future.

● Looking back over your past, there may be a point at which you need to be repentant for your part in what went wrong. Share this with one of your church leaders so that they can help you.

● Forgive others. Even if those who have wronged us do not want our forgiveness, it is important to be sure that we hold no bitterness against them. Again, if you find you've been hanging on to feelings of anger and bitterness, talk and pray that through with one of the church leaders.

MAINTAINING THE COMMITMENT

Our society has trivialised love. When people go to marriage counsellors after eighteen months of marriage and say, 'We're not in love any more,' what they mean

is, 'He/she doesn't make me feel gooey inside any more.'
Of course they're no longer in love in that sense! I don't
know of one married couple who could honestly say
that they're always 'in love' with each other in that
warm, sentimental-glow sense. If we're honest, there
have probably been many times this week when we
have felt pretty unloving towards our partner – something they did or didn't do – again; a cutting word that
was spoken, a broken promise.

Did you know that married couples speak to each
other in code? In our household, the code goes something like this:

> *Me:*   How are you?
> (Meaning: I think I've blown it again.)

> *Jan:*   Fine.
> (Meaning: Awful. And it's all your
> fault!)

> *Me:*   Do you want to talk about it?
> (Meaning: Well at least *I'm* making an
> effort to be grown up!)

> *Jan:*   No.
> (Meaning: Yes.)

Or take this example:

Jan: Steve, will you take the rubbish out, please?
(Meaning: Now, before the dust cart comes.)

Me: Yes, of course. (Meaning: Yes, of course; perhaps this afternoon.)

Another common variation on this one is:

Me: Don't worry about the washing up. (Meaning: I suppose it's my turn again.)

Jan: Oh, are you happy to do it, then? (Meaning: Great! If Steve does that now, I can get on with preparing for tonight's dinner party.)

Me: Yes, that's fine. Leave it to me. (Meaning: I'll do it tomorrow morning.)

Let's be realistic. The gooey sort of love doesn't last. Real love is a deep and faithful commitment to a person that persists in spite of the coded ways we talk and relate to each other. So what can we do to help maintain that commitment?

• Work at it! Marriage is jolly hard work. Staying happily married isn't something that just happens – unlike falling in love.

• Put your marriage relationship before every other

relationship – including your relationship with your work.

● If you or your partner are under stress and it's telling on your marriage, don't delay in getting others to pray with you and for you.

● If your church offers an opportunity from time to time for partners to renew their marriage vows, take it! If your church doesn't do this, you could suggest to the leaders that it might be helpful to do so. Even if the church doesn't have a public service for couples to do this, dig out the order of service of your wedding, and go over the promises you made then. You can renew them on your own before God, and ask him to help you keep them.

5

A PASSION
FOR
JUSTICE

'A trail-blazing burglar broke into a vast mansion on millionaires' row in June 1982 at Bel Air, Los Angeles. While on a sack-filling tour of this palatial structure, he went through the ballroom into the hall, down the escalators to the single-lane swimming arbour, up to the library across the dining-room, out of the annexe and into the conservatory containing sixty-three varieties of tropical plants and a cageful of sulphur-crested parrots.

Deciding that now was the time to make a quick exit, he went back through the dining-room, up to the gymnasium across the indoor tennis-court, down a spiral staircase to an enclosed patio with synchronized fountains, out of the cocktail lounge through junior's sound-proofed drum studio and back into the roomful of increasingly excited parrots who normally see nobody from one day to the next.

Panicking slightly, he ran back towards the library, through swing doors into a gallery containing the early works of Jackson Pollock, out through the kitchen across a jacuzzi enclosure and up two flights of stairs, at which point he became hysterical, ran outside along the balcony around the circular corridors, up more stairs, down the landing into the master bedroom and woke up the owners to ask them how to get out.

In order to spare him further distress, they arranged for a local policeman to escort him from the premises.' (From *The Return of Heroic Failures* by Stephen Pile, Harmondsworth: Penguin, 1989.)

Most of us have a strong sense of justice, and are delighted when a wrongdoer gets caught. Children have a very keen sense of justice. 'It's not fair!' is the wail of outrage and despair often heard among them as they play. That sense of justice persists into adult life and is the key to our making sense of life at all. If there was no punishment for doing wrong, or reward for doing right, there could be no order in society and, in the end, no purpose to life at all. When it seems that evil people are being allowed to get away with their crimes, and that the innocent and defenceless are suffering ever greater wrongs, we want to know why. What are the police up to? What are the courts doing about it? And why is God letting them get away with it?

A JUST GOD?

It was an issue that bothered the people of Malachi's day. They had all but given up on God. 'He's obviously not interested,' they said. 'He doesn't see or hear what's going on. He probably doesn't care any more – unless he's on the side of those with power.' And then God spoke to them through Malachi:

> 'You have wearied the Lord with your words.
> "How have we wearied him?" you ask.
> By saying, "All who do evil are good in the eyes of the Lord, and he is pleased with them" or "Where is the God of justice?"'
> *Malachi 2:17*

'What's the use of doing good when those who do bad get away with it? We do good and nothing happens;

we do bad and nothing happens. It doesn't seem to make any difference at all to God!' This was the nearest a Jew of Malachi's day could get to atheism. Asking, 'Where is the God of justice, who is supposed to be putting things right?' is the next best thing to saying, 'If there isn't a God of justice, there isn't a God at all.' Twentieth-century man tends to ask a slightly different question: 'If there is a God, how come there's all this suffering?' That is the great problem that makes us doubt the existence of God.

Throughout the Bible we find people looking at the injustices around them in the world and saying 'It's not fair!' And as we look round the world today we see evil world rulers, rampant terrorism, and terrible poverty and starvation as a result of evil people deliberately refusing food, clothing and water to their fellow creatures. Hundreds of thousands of people live and die in refugee camps in the most appalling conditions, because governments refuse to agree. Seeing all this we cry out to God to do something, to make things right.

But side by side with the demands from people in the Bible to know what God thinks he's doing, there is also a strong affirmation that God will one day sort it all out. In the King James' Version of the Bible, Psalm 37 begins, 'Fret not thyself because of evildoers.' And it goes on to say that evildoers will not go on getting away with it. They will get their just deserts. The God of all the world will see that right is seen to be right and wrong is seen to be wrong. It may have to wait until that great day at the end of time when all of us stand in front of the Almighty God and he finally says, 'Enough is enough.' Then all wrongs will finally be righted.

A PEOPLE CALLED TO BRING JUSTICE

Now, though, God calls his people to start doing what they can to bring about justice. Many of the things we have come to regard as our 'rights' today were won for us by the hard work of committed Christians. William Wilberforce and John Newton struggled politically and prayerfully to bring about the banning of the slave trade in this country, so ending a horrible form of injustice. Lord Shaftesbury campaigned year after year for the reduction of children's working hours in the mills, factories and pits of Britain when it was newly industrialised. God calls his people to be his agents of justice on earth. He does establish his righteousness when his body takes it seriously and does something about it.

To some extent we are culpable as a church world-wide for the lack of justice in the world today. If we were the church God intended us to be, his justice would reign in a way we would find simply incredible. But even if we were doing all we are supposed to, there would still be loose ends to be tied up, and they will be tied up on that great Day when Jesus comes again. This is exactly what Malachi was saying to the people of his day, speaking of the first and second comings of Christ almost as though they were rolled into one:

> ' "See, I will send my messenger, who will prepare the way before me. Then suddenly the Lord you are seeking will come to his temple; the messenger of the covenant, whom you desire, will come," says the Lord Almighty.'
>
> *Malachi 3:1*

Prepare the ground

Throughout the Old Testament there is constant reference to a messenger who will come immediately before the Lord himself comes. The messenger will prepare people to receive him. Isaiah writes:

> 'Prepare the way for the Lord;
> make straight in the wilderness
>   a highway for our God.

> Every valley shall be raised up,
>   every mountain and hill made low;
> the rough ground shall become level,
>   the rugged places a plain.'
>
> *Isaiah 40:3–4*

It's a lovely picture of huge, cavernous valleys being filled in with earth and great mountain ranges being levelled flat so that when the King comes he neither has to go on massive detours into the valleys or struggle over huge mountains. He can go straight to his people.

The classic example of the messenger who fulfils this prophecy is John the Baptist, who was the forerunner of Jesus. When he started preaching to the needy people in the first-century world he said, 'I am not the Christ, but am sent ahead of him' (John 3:28). He said he wasn't worthy even to untie the shoelaces of the one who was to come after him.

John was the wild man of the first century. A man who lived in the desert and fed on locusts and honey, and would leap out from boulders when people came down to the Jordan to do their weekly wash, and shout out, 'Repent!' Of course, they would be most upset at having their weekly laundry disturbed in this way, and they got a little frightened of him too. But John became a curiosity:

'What are you going to do today?'

'Well, we thought we'd go to see what John is up to. It's quite a good show really, if you get there early enough; but he'll be saying all sorts of things we don't understand.'

Great crowds would gather day after day and John would say, 'Someone holy and mighty is coming soon. Repent of your sins now, before it is too late. Change your minds and change your behaviour.' One day he saw a figure walking down towards the river and he pointed to him. As the huge crowd turned to look, John said, 'Behold, the Lamb of God who takes away the sin of the world.' Then Jesus came up to John and was baptised by him. Almost immediately, John recedes from the stage. From then on the Gospels take up the story of Jesus.

John was a forerunner, a preparer of the ground. God calls us, too, to prepare the ground for him so that he can move smoothly into people's lives. We can prepare the ground in two main ways.

In preaching and teaching

As we listen to God's word, week by week, it can help us to clear away the debris in our lives so that God has a clear pathway in. When we leave church thinking, 'I needed that this morning; that really spoke to me,' that's great! But it is only the ground being cleared. We then need to act on what we have heard and invite the King to come into our lives along that clear pathway. Many people who hear preaching, or read books or even the Bible, never get to the stage of welcoming in the King. They have got as far as the ground-clearing but their lives have not been materially changed.

By prayer

Even Jesus did not act in his ministry without preparing the ground first. He said, 'The Son can do nothing by himself; he can do only what he sees his Father doing' (John 5:19). He first looked for what God was already doing in people's lives, then he operated on the strength of what he saw. Jesus deliberately limited himself to working where the ground had been prepared. That has implications for us.

It has implications particularly for prayer, especially when we are involved in any sort of counselling ministry. When we are talking with others, it is important to be praying too, listening to what God is saying to them and discerning what he is doing in their lives. Otherwise we'll simply be coming out with our own good ideas. When we listen to what God is saying to these people, and hearing it in our spirits, we can pray for those people in line with God's will for them. Then we can be sure of our prayers being effective.

One reason why the Pentecostal revival happened, in the first decade of this century, was that the ground had been prepared. It didn't just happen by God saying, 'Let there be revival!' People had been meeting for months and years before, to fast, pray and seek God, and it was on the basis of that preparation that the Holy Spirit came, and what we know as the modern Pentecostal movement sprang out of it.

It is a principle that works in our own lives too. When we are prepared spiritually, when we have prayed and perhaps fasted, the Lord comes in a special way. Occasionally he will surprise us when we are unprepared, but generally speaking, God acts when there is a prepared heart to act into.

Welcome in the King

The problem with so many of us is that we are too busy for God, and see his coming into our lives as an intrusion rather than as a visit from a dear friend that we have been looking forward to for ages. A hymn by Isaac Watts, that we sometimes sing at Christmas, says:

'Joy to the world, the Lord is come;
Let earth receive her King!
Let every heart prepare him room
And heaven and nature sing.'

When we prepare him room in our hearts, he will come in and live there.

If Aunt Esmerelda is coming for the weekend, or the grandparents are going to be around or some other visitors are coming, you've got to do something with the spare room! You hurry around, get the sheets out, air the room and make sure the cobwebs don't look too obvious. And what about meals? What food do you need to get in? We do a lot of planning.

If special guests are coming we do even more – searching through the cupboards for the serviettes that must be here somewhere. We dust down the best china that hasn't been used since the day after we were married, and all the special things start to come out.

I remember the day Janet came out of hospital having given birth to Bethany. I had festooned the front of the house with toilet paper and various other things, spelling out, 'Welcome home, mother and baby'; 'We love you'; and all those kind of things. As Jan got out of the car, with the three-day old baby in her arms, she was terribly excited to come home to all this slightly soggy toilet paper! Well, maybe it was the feeling that she was loved and that I wanted her back home, that pleased her, rather than the amateur decorations!

God wants us to prepare for the coming of a very special guest, himself. Yet most of us go through our Christian lives fairly unprepared, and if we have an encounter with the living God at all, it's a haphazard, chance event. We may happen to bump into him in the street of our life – a casual contact in the passing busyness of everyday concerns, rather than a welcome into a home lovingly prepared for him.

A GOD WHO REFINES AND PURIFIES

God's coming into our lives may be welcomed by us, but it may not be an altogether comfortable experience:

> 'But who can endure the day of his coming? Who can stand when he appears? For he will be like a refiner's fire or a launderer's soap. He will sit as a refiner and purifier of silver; he will purify the Levites and refine them like gold and silver. Then the Lord will have men who will bring offerings in righteousness, and the offerings of Judah and Jerusalem will be acceptable to the Lord, as in days gone by, as in former years.'
>
> *Malachi 3:2–4*

Gold and silver were refined in furnaces so that any impurities were 'boiled away' and all that was left was the pure silver or gold. Launderer's soap wasn't so much a fourth-century BC Camay, as a bleaching agent. It was a whitener used to make dirty, grimy material gleaming white again. A fourth-century BC commercial for launderer's soap would show a stunning difference between the 'before' and 'after' look of the clothes being whitened!

In the same way, the coming of the Lord to his people would involve the purging away of all that was wrong in them, and the purifying of all that was right and good. It was a process that would be aimed particularly at the Levites, the priests and teachers of the Law.

Jesus was that purifier, the Lord who came to his temple and found the priests of his day full of impurities and corruption. When he spoke in public to the Pharisees, Jesus didn't mince his words. Here was no gentle, warm glow to make them feel comfortable, but a blaze of fire that was intended to sift the evil from the good: 'You are hypocrites! You put massive burdens on people when God didn't put those burdens on them. You claim extortionate amounts of the tithe for yourselves instead of releasing it so that the people can be cared for properly. You say to people, "Don't bother to spend your money in looking after your elderly relatives, give it to us instead and God will take care of them." You are like tombs that look lovely and white on the outside, but inside are full of stinking rotten matter!' (See Matthew 23.)

And when Jesus comes the second time, to bring to an end the world as we know it, he will do precisely the same thing. Soon after his harsh words to the Pharisees, Matthew records Jesus talking about the end of time, when the 'sheep' will be separated from the 'goats'. The good from the worthless.

The work of the Holy Spirit

This refining work is also the role of the Holy Spirit. John writes that, when the Holy Spirit comes, 'he will convict the world of guilt in regard to sin and righteousness and judgment' (John 16:8). That's why he's called the 'holy' Spirit, not the 'power' Spirit or the 'love' Spirit, or the 'joy' Spirit, even though he gives his love, joy and power. When he comes into our lives he convicts us of our sin, and that is why any experience of the Holy Spirit – be it called Baptism, the Fullness or the Filling – which does not involve an experience of our own sinfulness and unworthiness, is rarely a genuine experience. The Holy Spirit cannot come without his holiness. He is like the launderer's soap and the refiner's fire which burns away the rubbish in our lives.

How easy it is for us to be thrown! To have our backs put out, or be offended, or react in an immature, childish way. We are easily thrown by changes just in our routine! We sometimes think we've got it all together, spiritually, that we're walking with God. But then someone makes a critical comment which we take ever so personally, and suddenly we're moody and immature children again. Why? Because there is still enough grot in our lives for the devil to get his hooks into. God's job is to refine us to get rid of all the mud that clings to us, so that when the devil throws his grappling irons towards us, his little hooks just slide off again. There should be no mud or dirt in our lives for them to grip hold of. But as long as we are unrefined the devil's claws have got something to grip into.

And then he starts to churn us up emotionally, because when we are churned up emotionally we act irrationally and say things we don't mean. With just a bit of stirring, the devil can make us blow everything up out of proportion, and then his work of wreaking havoc in our lives is straightforward. That's why we need to have all the dirt refined out of us. We are called to be holy.

There's a lovely hymn which traces the struggle we have in releasing our grip on our 'rights', and the unholy things we want to cling on to, and handing them over to God instead. The line at the end of verse one goes, 'More of self and less of thee.' The end of the next verse says, 'Less of self and more of thee', and then the very last line of the hymn is, 'None of self and all of thee.' It is a little like the caterpillar and the butterfly where, in a sense, the caterpillar has to die in order to release the butterfly. That which is worldly and corrupting in us has to die before Christ can be fully formed in us instead.

GOD IS THE JUDGE OF SOCIETY

When the Lord returns again, it is not just individuals who will be judged, but society as a whole:

> ' "So I will come near to you for judgment. I will be quick to testify against sorcerers, adulterers and perjurers, against those who defraud labourers of their wages, who oppress the widows and the fatherless, and deprive aliens of justice, but do not fear me," says the Lord Almighty.'
>
> *Malachi 3:5*

When God says that he will be 'quick' to judge, he

doesn't mean he's going to make a snap decision. The word used is an unusual Hebrew word that also conveys the meaning, 'expert'. How can 'quick' mean the same as 'expert'? Well, it's not as silly as it first sounds.

If you went out to your car now, looked at it and found you had a flat tyre, you'd probably try to get it pumped up again. Suppose you couldn't, because it was too badly damaged? You'd need to change it. And for that, you need the right tools. Someone who has got the right tools and has done the job many times is going to change it much more quickly than someone with none of the tools or skills! If you stand around, kick the wheel and try to get the nuts off with your finger nails, it will take you an age to get the wheel changed! An expert does the job quickly.

A few years ago, Jan and I went to the Ideal Home Exhibition in London. We wandered around and saw a number of demonstrations of things that the home Should Not Be Without. One of them was an amazing grater. All you did was to rub your salad vegetables up and down on it, and the shreds would magically appear, beautifully designed and artistically arranged. It was amazing, and was an absolute bargain! So we bought one. After we got home we enthusiastically had a go with the new toy – but nothing like the magnificent salads appeared! It took hours of practice before anything like the right shapes began to emerge.

An expert produces things quickly. God is quick to judge because he is the expert. He knows all about the people he is judging. He is quick, not because he is casual, or unthinking or superficial, but because he has perfect knowledge.

Four areas of judgment

Malachi warns that every area of life is going to be examined by God. The examples he gives represent the four major areas:

• *Its spiritual life*. Everything that is corrupt spiritually will be judged: the 'sorcerers', the occult and the misleading.

• *Its moral life*. Those who by immorality wreak havoc in society, breaking up homes and destroying the security of children, will be judged.

• *Its ethical life*. 'Perjurers' are those who bend the truth in order to make others think they are better than they are. All lies, deception and deceit will be judged.

• *Its social justice*. How does our society treat its poor? What provision does it make for them? How does it care for the sick, the mentally ill, the disabled? What are we doing about the scourge of unemployment? Where is justice and fairness in our life together as a society? These are questions that God will ask of us and our leaders.

Stepping into the refiner's fire

The Lord calls us to step into the refiner's fire. If we are to be able to call society back to God's standards of holiness and justice, we must first allow his Holy Spirit to work in us. We have to be willing to let go of those areas of impurity in our lives, deliberately turning our backs on them and renouncing them. And we need to let the Holy Spirit fully into every corner of our hearts, to shine his spotlight onto the dirt that remains and to purge it out. And then we need both to speak out in society, and to act, working to clear out the evils we find and to put positive alternatives in their place.

6

INTEGRITY

WITH

MONEY

Pastor: You say you can't give to the church because you owe everyone else. Don't you feel that you owe the Lord something?

Church member: Yes, of course I do. But he isn't pushing me like the others!

At a social event one man told another: 'I've met you before but I can't place you. Or perhaps you just look like someone I see around a lot. I can't place him but I know I don't like him. Isn't that strange? He's someone I resent – but I can't think who he is. Isn't that odd?'

The other man answered, 'Nothing strange about it! It's me you've seen a lot and I know why you resent me. For two years I used to pass the collection plate round in church!'

Money is a tricky subject to talk about publicly, especially from the pulpit. Give just one sermon a year on our financial responsibilities to the church, and people resent it and say, 'The church is always asking for money!' God introduced the subject of money to his people in a very different way:

> ' "I the Lord do not change. So you, O descendants of Jacob, are not destroyed. Ever since the time of your forefathers you have turned away from my decrees and have not kept them. Return to me, and I will return to you," says the Lord Almighty.
> "But you ask, 'How are we to return?' " '
>
> *Malachi 3:6–7*

THE ULTIMATE SECURICOR

Time and again the Israelites broke their covenant with God. Yet he remained faithful to them. Despite the punishments he sent their way, he never gave up on them. He held open the invitation to return to him, to restore their relationship with him of love and trust.

Because God does not change, we have a marvellous security as Christians. If we have given our lives to Jesus Christ and he has come to live inside us, we form part of the great Kingdom of God that cannot be shaken because it is ruled by a King who will never change and whose power will never be diminished. He is the ultimate Securicor.

It is good to know that in our volatile world. As we look at the TV or read the papers, we see the moods of international politics fluctuating, and learn to accept that major changes in the political geography of the world can take place overnight. It can be frightening to think about. Yet the Christian can have the inner certainty that the God who holds us in the hollow of his hand will not change. 'Jesus Christ is the same yesterday, today and for ever' (Hebrews 13:8). Because of that, you and I can face the future with confidence.

What is true on the international scale is also true on the personal scale. I suspect that most of us are affected by our moods, to a greater or lesser extent. The state of our digestive system can determine the way we react to an innocent question someone asks us. Whether or not we enjoyed breakfast can affect our mood for the rest of the day. If someone cuts us up when we're driving, it can make us irritable and grouchy. God has none of those mood swings, but is steady and constant, always ready to receive us. So when we come to him in the evening and say, 'Lord, I want to talk about my day,' he doesn't say, 'Keep it to yourself! You think *your* day was bad? You should have seen *mine*! I've had another uprising in the Middle East to deal with, a famine going on in Africa, some delicate negotiations to oversee in the White House...' God may be grieved by what is happening in the world, but he isn't thrown by it. He doesn't get moody or fed up but is constantly available to the searching believer.

The fault is on our side. It is we who are praising the Lord one minute, and the next being down in the dumps, wanting nothing to do with other Christians! In God is total security and reliability.

'So', he asks, 'what's holding you back from me? Why don't you trust me?'

'Holding back?' his people ask in amazement. 'We're not holding back from you!'

'Yes you are,' he replies. 'The proof of the fact that you don't trust me is that you won't trust me with your money. In fact, not only do you not trust me with your money, you're actually defrauding me of what is rightfully mine!'

> ' "Will a man rob God? Yet you rob me.
>   "But you ask, 'How do we rob you?'
>   "In tithes and offerings. You are under a curse – the whole nation of you – because you are robbing me. Bring the whole tithe into the storehouse, that there may be food in my house. Test me in this," says the Lord Almighty, "and see if I will not throw open the floodgates of heaven and pour out so much blessing that you will not have room enough for it. I will prevent pests from devouring your crops, and the vines in your fields will not cast their fruit," says the Lord Almighty. "Then all the nations will call you blessed, for yours will be a delightful land," says the Lord Almighty.'   *Malachi 3:8–12*

The word translated 'rob' means 'plunder'. It's a very strong accusation. It's the idea of coshing a Securicor guard on the head when he's loading money out of the bank into a van. It means taking by force what is not yours.

Yet there is another side to the picture. 'Will a man rob God?' asks the Lord. 'Don't be so ridiculous,' comes the reply. You might as well suggest to an ant that it gets a little black mask with two eye holes, tucks a cosh under one leg and a torch under another, and creeps up on an elephant to mug it. Even though he bashes away at the elephant's big toe, the elephant won't even know he's there. 'And can insignificant, puny human beings plunder the God of the universe?' asks Malachi.

There is a barb in his question. It might be impossible, but the Israelites are certainly trying it on! In two ways they are defrauding God of what is rightfully his.

VALUE PEOPLE ABOVE MONEY

Their culture was materialistic, as is ours, with a sick attitude to money. At a conservative estimate, about fifty million pounds is gambled away each year on the Grand National – and that's only the officially placed bets. What could fifty million pounds achieve if all those people chose to put their betting money to a different cause? What sort of society is it that can encourage that amount to be squandered, while at the same time saying that little can be done about the lack of housing and health care?

One night I had the dubious privilege of walking the floors of the casino in Monte Carlo. Wandering around the tables, I saw gambler after gambler throw dice to the end of a table, or bet on the spin of a wheel. I saw people playing cards and losing hundreds of francs. The whole atmosphere of the place is depressing and heavy. It's supposed to be fun! It was anything but that. I left very depressed about the kind of world that encourages such incredible waste, and encourages people to believe that trying to get something for nothing is the way to spend their leisure time.

The Grand National and the Casino are simply indicators of the grasping spirit that wants more and more, and that regards the needs of the poor, alienated and suffering as far less important than a few moments' thrill at watching the horses or spinning the wheel.

Malachi condemns the people of God for an attitude to money that is basically unhealthy. In our society it is easy to think that giving to charity has increased over recent years because of the efforts of groups like Band Aid, Live Aid and Sport Aid. But if you read the annual report and accounts of some long-standing missionary societies and Christian agencies, you will discover that what has happened is simply that the amount of money they receive has decreased in corresponding measure to the amount the newer ones have netted. The overall level of giving in this country hasn't really changed very much.

We need to watch it in the church, too. Although we can criticise the nation, the spirit of the age fills the Church of Jesus. Our attitude to money becomes warped, and our priorities become increasingly materialistic and decreasingly those of the Kingdom of God. It is easy to be robbed of a sense of the Kingdom at work, actively and successfully in the world, by a cultural system that values money and things more highly than people.

VALUE GOD ABOVE MONEY

Malachi's second call was to a rethink of the value they put on God. His accusation was that they were not keeping the law on tithing, that is, committing to God one tenth of all their income, whether financial or in kind with wheat and corn. Because the tithe was not being paid, there was no way the priests and other temple staff could carry out their jobs properly. The priests were not allowed to own their own land, so they were dependent on the people supplying the basic necessities of life for them. Because the money wasn't there, the priests' families were going hungry and the whole temple 'system' was under pressure. 'That can't be right,' says Malachi. 'How come you've got money to spend on all sorts of things that you want, but God's house remains impoverished, empty and weak?'

God's work through the church

Here we are, 2400 years later, and still the work of the Kingdom of God is hindered through lack of finances! Ask anyone involved in evangelism – Christian publishers, broadcasters and missionaries – and you will hear the same story: 'Barring a miracle, we are not going to make the budget again this year.' Sometimes missionary societies don't get the vision right, and that is why the money isn't provided for their work. But nine times out of ten their vision is right, their goals for development and ministry are sound, but they cannot go in to take the ground because God's people, on whom they rely, are not giving as they should be.

I had the privilege, while I was in Monte Carlo, of talking to Christians who have set up a broadcasting station there. Many of them had been thrown out of old-style Communist countries or had escaped under threat of death, or had suffered torture for their faith. Yet as they walked through the streets of Monte Carlo and looked up at the opulent buildings and glamorous sights, they could honestly say it had no appeal for them. Their faith in the Lord was so rich that material things seemed utterly worthless in comparison.

Our own priorities

When John Wesley went to Oxford as a student in the early years of the eighteenth century, he lived on twenty-eight pounds a year. It would be pretty difficult to do that now! But at one point his salary was doubled and he still lived on twenty-eight pounds a year – he gave the rest away. In about the twentieth year of his ministry, his writing and the patronage he was gaining meant that he was receiving an annual income of thousands of pounds. Yet he still lived on just £28 a year.

Admittedly, he didn't have a problem with inflation in those days. Yet it was still a remarkable commitment.

Today, our finances are much more complicated. We have family responsibilities and pressures, and the practicalities of insurance and mortgages. But the principle is still a crucial one to hold on to: we rob God and we rob his kingdom if we are not generous supporters of his work.

What can we do about this accusation?

• Assess what money you *need*, and be clear about what are really unnecessary luxuries that you could go without.

Do you know what wastage is? Wastage is what someone else spends their money on! It's never something I spend *my* money on! I can say to Janet, 'For goodness' sake! Not another dress? I mean, you had one last year!' I can make her feel incredibly worldly for buying new clothes or cosmetics. 'Do you really need to give money to that wretched Avon lady?! It's just so worldly!' Of course, the money I spend on books is easy to justify. That's 'spiritual'!

God is calling us to look at the way we are using our *own* finances and resources, not anyone else's, and to ask ourselves, 'Is that really right?'

• Aim to give a tenth of your income to the work of the church. A tithe was a tenth – that was what the people owed God. A gift to God was anything in excess of that sum. People differ today about whether that is still the sum Christians should be giving, but I have always found it a good guideline.

• Trust God. 'Test me in this,' says the Lord, 'and see if I will not open the floodgates of heaven and pour out so much blessing that you will not have room enough for it.' Now I have heard people talk about giving and tithing as though it is a direct equation: give 'x' amount to God and he will give you 'x' plus 'y' in return. Giving on that basis ceases to be the duty or love gift it was meant to be and turns into a mercenary, commercial deal instead. It is simply an unbiblical approach to money. I give because God tells me to give; blessing is the result of obedience.

I know of many couples who were once in a real mess financially. Then they talked and prayed together about it and they decided that, for the first time in their married lives, they would give a tithe. God would have first claim on their money, then they would prioritise how to spend what was left. And these couples would affirm that God has never let them down. They have been able to meet their needs, despite giving away that amount. God has honoured their commitment and their desire to use their money responsibly.

• God doesn't demand that we give beyond our means. We need to be sensitive to his Spirit, to give as we feel we ought to, taking into account the responsibility he has also given us to feed, clothe and care for our families.

THE RESOLVE TO ACT

'Then those who feared the Lord talked with each other, and the Lord listened and heard. A scroll of remembrance was written in his presence concerning those who feared the Lord and honoured his name.

"They will be mine," says the Lord Almighty, "in the day when I make up my treasured possession. I will spare them, just as in compassion a man spares his son who serves him. And you will again see the distinction between the righteous and the wicked, between those who serve God and those who do not." '

Malachi 3:16–18

The need to listen

After Malachi's challenge to the priests and people, they decided they needed to do something about it. 'Those who feared the Lord' held a meeting and discussed what it would involve to put things right, and how they should go about it.

If God has been speaking to you through the words of Malachi, as you have read them in this book, don't dismiss his voice. Share your thoughts with other Christian friends and ask for their reactions to what you think God is saying to you. Then go on to what the people of Malachi's day did next: action!

The resolve to act

You may have been challenged about one or more of the areas we have looked at so far in this book: your worship, your representation of God as his priest, your personal relationships, the part you are playing in bringing about a more just society, or your use of your money and things. Look back over those chapters that concerned you most, and decide now exactly what you are going to do to put things right. Prayerfully, draw up a plan of action for yourself. Then share your decisions with a friend and ask for his or her prayer support and practical encouragement to stick to it.

The affirmation of God

We noticed at the beginning of Malachi that God does not condemn for long before bringing renewed affirmation of his people and his love for them. That comes out again here. First, God affirms that his people are totally secure with him; he never changes. Then he challenges them to take him up on that and entrust themselves and their money to him. Now again he wants them to know that they are his treasured possession. Whether or not they have much in the way of this world's goods, they are themselves of great value to God. Despite their failures in the past, he will see that they get into heaven, not just sliding in at the back, but being borne in with triumph as the crown jewels!

God knows our situation. He knows that life gets rough and dispiriting. He knows that it is a struggle

120

for us to keep putting him first. He takes note when Christians go without for years, in order to provide for others. He knows when they clothe others and go about badly dressed themselves. He knows when they are providing the means for others to be housed, yet suffering poor housing themselves. One day, all of that will be recompensed in heaven. Those who love the Lord and choose to identify with him here in his poverty, will be received by him as honoured guests at the feast at the end of time.

7

A
NEW
FREEDOM

I remember a time when I was in the States. I had just said goodbye to Jan and was about to drive to the airport to go on a trip to Israel. On the way to the airport I called in at my apartment to pick up one or two things – I thought I might need the odd shirt for a fortnight away. But the moment I stepped inside I developed the most awful pain in my side, so bad that I couldn't even stand. Fortunately, my future mother-in-law was there, and we phoned a doctor friend in the church to get some advice.

'Yes,' he said, 'It sounds bad. Drive into the surgery.' And he put the phone down, without telling us where the surgery was! So I frantically looked through the church membership list to try to find out if his office was listed. It was. So, grasping a map and this huge, twenty-thousand-member list, I climbed into the front seat next to Jan's mum. As she drove, I sat hunched over in pain, giving directions: 'It's left here, right here . . .' We went right the way round north Dallas. At last we arrived – and the first thing they wanted to know was how I was going to pay! Well, things got sorted out in the end. The pain was diagnosed as kidney stones and I got some helpful treatment.

For the whole of that journey I was desperate to get there! All the time I'd been thinking, '*Surely* it must be just here! Just round the next corner . . . it *must* be!' In America the blocks are numbered, so you can tell when you're getting near your destination. Say you have to get to block 20, and you're now at block 40. You count every block: '39, 38, 37 . . . we're getting there! 27, 26 . . . not far to go now . . . !'

This was the sort of longing desperation that the Old Testament prophets felt for 'the day of the Lord', the day when he would come and sort out the mess the world had got into. It was a day Malachi longed for too:

' "Surely the day is coming; it will burn like a furnace. All the arrogant and every evildoer will be stubble, and that day that is coming will set them on fire," says the Lord Almighty. "Not a root or a branch will be left to them. But as for you who revere my name, the sun of righteousness will rise with healing in its wings. And you will go out and leap like calves released from the stall. Then you will trample down the wicked; they will be ashes under the soles of your feet on the day when I do these things," says the Lord Almighty.' *Malachi 4:1–3*

'Surely the day is coming,' says Malachi, 'when God will at last intervene, and the world's pain, injustice and corruption will be dealt with!'

LONGING FOR FULFILMENT

It is a longing we share today. When Malachi and the other prophets spoke of the day of the Lord, they saw two times compressed into one – the time when Jesus first came to this earth, and the day when he will return a second time. They longed for two things to happen: the law of God to become a part of his people, 'written on their hearts' as Jeremiah had put it, and they longed for all society's rottenness to get sorted out.

When Jesus came, these two longings began to be

fulfilled. He came to give us his Holy Spirit. That means we can truly begin to think, feel and act like Jesus himself. And it also means we can begin to begin to do some of his purifying work, acting as salt and light in society.

I sometimes have the opportunity of counselling many non-Christians at big events. One one occasion, after a seminar called Agnostics Anonymous, one man came up to me and said, 'I'm really enjoying it here but, tell me, how do I know this Jesus?' He asked me while we were with a group of people, so I said that if he would give me ten minutes on his own I would answer him.

We met again the next day. He was a research scientist in his middle age, and we spent about an hour talking about all the questions of the universe and the God who made the world. He saw that the Christian view made sense of all this so, after a while asked, 'What are we waiting for?' 'Well, nothing,' I replied. So we went back to his chalet and sat on his bed with his wife, and we prayed that he would come to know Jesus as Saviour and Lord. He looked up from that prayer, his face transformed, and said something like, 'Now I know! My wife has been a Christian for ten years, and I've been to church with her every Sunday morning because she wanted me to go with her. But now I have stopped longing to know what on earth it was she had; now I know for myself!' For him, the frustrating time of waiting and puzzling was over.

It's not just people like this man who wait and wonder what it's all about. Many of us Christians come to church Sunday by Sunday and sit in on the worship, but we may be feeling, 'When is it going to feel real for me? When am I really going to know this Jesus?' Perhaps you have been a Christian for many years and have been longing to be filled with the power of the Holy Spirit, but don't quite know how to 'get hold' of it. You may be saying to yourself, 'Surely the day is coming when God will bless me?' Yes, he wants to come to bless you and fulfil your longings to know him better.

In the coming of Jesus, the prophets' time of waiting was over. And for all of us our time of waiting will be over when he returns for the second time.

THE CUTTING EDGE

There are some people who are not looking forward to that day. Ham and chicken pie sounds very nice, but not if you're a pig or a chicken! Whether we look forward to that day or not depends on our vantage point. If we're the kind of person Malachi mentions first, 'the arrogant and every evildoer', the day of the Lord will be our judgment day. But if we're a different sort of person, that day can hold no fear for us: 'But for you who revere my name, the sun of righteousness will rise with healing in its wings.'

All evil and all evil people will be as stubble in the fire, on that day. This is the cutting edge to the Old Testament message which we sometimes miss or try to soften in current Christian teaching. We tell people about God's love for them, and about how Jesus will give them peace and forgiveness if they come to him. We tell them how he will bring them into a new family and give them his Holy Spirit. All that is true, but the flip side of that coin, of which the prophets constantly remind us, is that God's holiness means that he is angry against sin.

God is not just a God of love. He is also a God of righteous anger. Far too often we allow people to get away with a caricature of Jesus as gentle and mild, going around being nice to children and widows, caring for those who were sick, and raising dead people back to life again. Of course he did do that. But he also strode into the temple in anger and overturned the tables of the money changers, pushing off the piles of money, scattering the pigeons, sheep and goats that were in the courtyard, and driving out the traders with a whip! Jesus was passionately loving, but also strongly angry against sin. The gospel is news of God's love. But its cutting edge is the news of God's judgment.

FREEDOM AND HEALING

'The sun of righteousness will rise with healing in its wings.' For centuries, people have believed that the sun's rays have healing properties. We now know it to be true, that vital vitamins are made in our skin only by the rays of the sun. There's something depressing about being shut up inside, perhaps having to study for exams, when the sun is shining brightly outside and the weather is warm and inviting.

From darkness to light

Malachi pictures the coming of the Lord as breaking into the dark cells of our lives and of our world, and letting us out into the warmth, freedom and sunshine. He uses a lovely picture of a calf that has been confined to a stall during the winter months longing to go out into the fields to see the spring. Suddenly the day comes when the door is unlocked and the calf is free to rush out into the sunlight, to gambol and dance around the field.

The revelation of Jesus brings the same sort of joyful and healing freedom to us. When we come to know him for the first time as adults, the contrast between the darkness and the sunlight is particularly strong – we have so much more of life behind us to contrast with the present.

From chains to freedom

The coming of the Lord into our lives brings us freedom from the chains that have bound us in the past. I once met a man who was confined to a wheelchair. One day he came to know Jesus for himself. He wasn't physically healed, but he was as free as any person can possibly be – all his bitterness and anger was released in prayer, and a freedom came into his life that you could almost touch. Looking at him still in his wheelchair you might say, 'That man's not free!' But he would call you a liar, because the greatest freedom of all had come to him – freedom from inner guilt and pain. It was marvellous to see him! He was just like a young child all over again. It was as if he had discovered a new lease of life, clapping at everything – even at the wrong time – warm and enthusiastic. Everything was new and fresh. Everything had suddenly become just great for him.

There is an old hymn which says, 'Something lives in every hue, Christless eyes have never seen.' The language may be a bit old fashioned, but it contains a lot of truth. When that man had his eyes opened to Jesus and had his bitterness washed away, something did live in every situation that he had never seen before. The world was richer, brighter, fuller. He was free for the first time.

From fear to confidence

Yet many of us have been like that calf, leaping out of the stall with great joy – only to hit our hoof on a stone and twist it. We've lost our nerve, hobbled back to the stable and never ventured out again. So now, when we look at the enthusiasm and joy of other young Christians discovering Christ for the first time, we say, Eeyore-like, 'Oh, that's just a stage they'll grow out of.'

The Lord wants to turn our fear and doubt into confidence. We all need to have our characters changed, and the Lord works with us to help us become like Christ – more loving, caring, holy, honest. But many of us also need to have our personalities changed by the

Lord, too. We need to be healed of the damage of past hurts, which have made us afraid and doubtful of our own abilities. The experiences and condemning words that have left us feeling failures and no-hopers, need to be seen for the lies they are. In their place, God wants us to see ourselves in our true light, that is, as he sees us. And that is as his precious, loved children. There's a song by D J Butler which describes this process of healing and change that happens as we come out of the stable and into the sunlight:

> *I will change your name*
>
> 'I will change your name.
> You shall no longer be called
>   Wounded, outcast,
>   Lonely or afraid.
>
> I will change your name.
> Your new name shall be:
>   Confidence, joyfulness,
>   Overcoming one,
>   Faithfulness, friend of God,
>   One who seeks My face.'
>
> *Copyright © 1987 Mercy*
> *Publishing/Thankyou Music*

God is looking through the stable door at you and saying, 'I've got a great list of things out here for you to explore and enjoy! Unlock the door and let the glorious light shine in, and come out to me and enjoy the freedom I want to give you!'

Freedom from sin and evil

Part and parcel of our complete freedom at the end of time, will be the destruction of all that is evil, and the wiping out of all our sinful traits. The stones that twist our ankles now will be gone then. It won't be possible to run out of the stall only to find ourselves charged by a mad bull! The world will be a place of total safety: ' "you will trample down the wicked; they will be ashes under the soles of your feet on the day when I do these things," says the Lord Almighty.'

The Old Testament writers aren't squeamish about evil, the way we tend to be today. The psalmists in particular didn't beat about the bush when they spoke about evil people: 'Lord, get 'em! Lord, smash 'em up! I hate them, because they hate you!' Today we're much more sophisticated, far nicer: 'Lord, convict them!'

At least the Old Testament writers had a strong hatred of evil. They saw in the raw the devastation it brought to people's lives. We need to watch that we don't tolerate sin too easily today, pooh-poohing it, treating it lightly or making excuses for it. The Lord himself does not treat it lightly. One day he will make an end of Satan, the serpent, and all his wiles. The evil influence which Satan and the powers of darkness exert over the earth now will one day be gone for ever. There will be a new heaven and a new earth, in which only goodness and righteousness shall reign. Then we and the whole creation will be truly free for the first time, and go leaping into the new, open and clean world 'like calves released from the stall.'

8
REFUSE
TO BE
AVERAGE

Benjamin Disraeli said, 'As a general rule, the most successful man in life is the man who has the best information.' He was only partly right. The best information isn't much use unless you act on it!

At the end of Spring Harvest, I sometimes think that there has been just too much information for some folk to take in. It's a case of information overload. What am I going to do with all those notes? Now that I've been to my forty-fifth seminar in a week, how am I going to be able to use all the information I've gleaned? It would take a good six months to put one tenth of it into practice – and the next six months to prepare for next Spring Harvest!

GROW IN WHAT YOU KNOW

It we are to be successful in our Christian lives, we need to make our knowledge real by living it out. 'Remember!' says Malachi. 'Don't gain new insights and knowledge just to forget it all again. Grow in what you know. Refuse to be average!'

> ' "Remember the law of my servant Moses, the decrees and laws I gave him at Horeb for all Israel." ' *Malachi 4:4*

This is a kind of summary of the message of all of the prophets. Their task was to point people back to the laws and teaching God had given them through Moses at the outset of their life together as a nation. 'Remember' is also the key word throughout the book of Deuteronomy. It occurs there about twelve times, always at major points in the people's experience of God. They were to take to heart the things that they learnt at those times, and not let the lessons slip from their minds.

Malachi reminds the people that the day of the Lord is coming. 'In view of that,' he asks them, 'how do you think you ought to be living now?' The obvious answer is, 'In a way which will please him.'

When we feel we are not growing as Christians,

the problem is often not that we need to discover new truths, but that we need to act on the old truths. Yes, we do need new experiences of God, but we need to enter into the joy of the old experiences as well.

Sometimes we can hear too much preaching and read too many Christian books! We can try to take in too much new information before we have properly digested what we have already heard and read. Perhaps we have known some biblical truths for years, but are still not living in the light of them. We need to grow in what we know, by putting it into practice.

START IN YOUR OWN FAMILY

The difference that Jesus makes in our lives should be seen most clearly in the way we live with those closest to us, our families:

> ' "See, I will send you the prophet Elijah before that great and dreadful day of the Lord comes. He will turn the hearts of the fathers to their children, and the hearts of the children to their fathers; or else I will come and strike the land with a curse." ' *Malachi 4:5–6*

Most commentators think the mention of Elijah is a

reference to the ministry of John the Baptist. God's messengers – whether Elijah, John the Baptist, Jesus himself or us as Jesus' disciples – have a crucial job to do: that of healing and renewing family bonds. When Jesus comes into our lives, with all his purity, power and healing, it should make a difference to our families.

The most crucial way he will do that is to help us 'turn our hearts towards our children.' We need to give time to our families, both 'quality' and 'quantity' time. Some of us are so busy with work or church that our husbands, wives or children don't get what they need either from us or from the Lord.

My experience of family life as a leader is probably fairly typical of other leaders' lives. I spend at least twenty minutes a day at home, snatching something to eat before running out to do some more counselling or speaking. Once when I was sitting reading my Bible, trying to prepare for a talk, and with my coat on ready to go. My young daughter, Bethany, came up to me and pulled the edges of my coat. 'Coat off!' she said. 'I can't take my coat off; I'm not staying!' I explained. So then she asked, 'Daddy reading Bible?' 'Yes.' 'Daddy put Bible away!' Frantically, I said, 'No! I can't do that!' So she took the Bible, closed it and put it on one side.

Then she gave me *Jane goes to Noddyland*, or something like that, and said, 'Daddy read this!' So I read it to her – at about a hundred miles an hour – and rushed out to my engagement.

What are we teaching our children about God by the amount of time we spend with them? Are they growing up to hate the Bible for keeping them away from Mummy or Daddy? Are they developing a deep resentment against the church because all their other friends are out at the seaside on a Sunday morning and they're struck in a dreary old building for hours on end? Are they learning to resent people coming into our house because they take up all Mum and Dad's time and mean no bedtime story? We need to be very careful that we are not always too busy for our children, but make their well-being our priority.

Part of the secret is to work to God's timetable rather than our own. If our children need us to minister to them – or just to go for a walk with them or play with them – we should see that as God's work, every bit as much as preaching to 1000 people. God's values are not always the same as ours! We might think it is better to spend ten hours preparing a sermon; God might think it would be time far better spent taking the family out for the day.

We want our children's hearts to be turned towards us, don't we? There's usually not too much trouble with the younger ones, but it's when they reach the impossibly awkward teenage years that we fear they are turning away from us. One mother ruefully confided to me, 'My daughter's at the teenage rebellion stage.' 'What's so unusual about that?' I asked. 'Well,' she said, 'she's only six!' If we want our children's hearts to be turned towards us, and to our Lord, what are we doing to turn our hearts towards them?

THE ONLY ALTERNATIVE

The last verse of Malachi, the last book of the Old Testament, is devastating: '. . . or I will come and strike the land with a curse.' This is not God being vindictive and angry. It is, rather, God pointing out the only possible alternative to living his way. We will not be able to avoid bringing sorrow and trouble on ourselves. The unspoken message is, 'Come back to me.' A stark way to end the Old Testament.

Yet if we look on to the last verses in the New Testament, we have the same sense of expectation, the same warnings of the alternative, and the same invitation to return to the Lord:

' "Behold, I am coming soon! My reward is with me, and I will give to everyone according to what he has done . . .

"Blessed are those who wash their robes, that they may have the right to the tree of life and may go through the gates into the city. Outside are the dogs, those who practise magic arts, the sexually immoral, the murderers, the idolaters and everyone who loves and practises falsehood . . .

"I, Jesus, have sent my angel to give you this testimony for the churches . . ."

The Spirit and the bride say, "Come!" And let him who hears say, "Come!" Whoever is thirsty, let him come; and whoever wishes, let him take the free gift of the water of life.'

Revelation 22:12–17

The Lords hold out two alternatives to us: life or death, judgment or grace. Let us choose life!

OTHER BOOKS IN THIS SERIES

Pioneers or Settlers? Exodus: Adventurous faith for today (Philip Mohabir)

God of New Beginnings: Matthew 1–4 in today's world (Roger Sainsbury)

Thirsty for God: Matthew 5–7: Jesus' teaching for today (Stephen Gaukroger)

Drawing Power: Living out Acts in today's world (Derek Prime)

People Under Pressure: 2 Corinthians: Strategy for stress (Michael Cole)

Open to Others: Ephesians: Overcoming barriers in today's church (Colin Buchanan)

Growing in Christ: 1 Thessalonians: Steps to Christian maturity (Paul Marsh)

Growing Your Gifts: 2 Timothy: Ministry in today's world (Stephen Gaukroger)